Bill & Sandy   12-29-04

Enjoy 50 years of Memories

John E. Ascuaga

Bill & Sandy,
Hope you enjoy this
as much as we do!

Michonne Ascuaga

Bill and Sandy,

Best Wishes!

Stephen

50 Years of Memories

1955

John Ascuaga's

Nugget

50

2005

Foreword

I remember the first day we opened the Nugget. It was a bright, clear day on March 17, 1955. The Nugget has grown a lot since that day. The success we've had stems from the strong values my parents taught me: honesty and integrity. It is with these values that we built the Nugget into what it is today, and that my children, Michonne and Stephen, will take it into the future.

50 Years of Memories is filled with photos and represents the hard work and dedication of countless people. It is not just about me, the Nugget or Sparks, but about the thousands of talented employees that the Nugget has been blessed with over the years.

I have always said that it is our employees who make us stand out from all the other casinos and restaurants; they are what make John Ascuaga's Nugget a success. My proudest achievement is that for 50 years I have been able to work alongside them, as an employee of the Nugget.

In 50 Years of Memories, you will watch the Nugget grow from a 60-seat coffee shop into one of Northern Nevada's largest casino/resorts. If you are a long-time customer, I hope that this book will bring back fond memories as it has for me. If not, I hope this book will give you and your family some insight to the Nugget's rich and colorful history.

The photos used for this book come from The Reno Gazette-Journal, the Nugget's marketing department, The Nevada Historical Society, employees and from our family's personal albums. Fifty years in business has created countless memories and narrowing those down to 143 pages was difficult, but I think we have done a pretty good job. In fact I would have to say that it is near perfect...

John J. Ascuaga

Acknowledgments

We are pleased to present "John Ascuaga's Nugget, 50 Years of Memories."
A lot has happened over six decades, leading from humble beginnings on
March 17, 1955, to a commanding presence on the Sparks skyline. This
pictorial history book touches proudly on it all.

"50 YEARS OF MEMORIES" PROJECT TEAM

- Beth Cooney
- Frankie Vigil
- Thomas G. McGuire
- Christine Thompson
- Cami Kaiser
- Mikalee Dahle, Gaye Delaplane, Mel Shields and John Trent — Writers
- Matt Lauc — Cover Design
- Mary Henry and Madeline Gausted — Contributors

THE ASCUAGA FAMILY

FRED HAMILTON, PUBLISHER, RENO GAZETTE-JOURNAL

NEVADA HISTORICAL SOCIETY

RENO GAZETTE-JOURNAL

RENO GAZETTE-JOURNAL CUSTOM PUBLISHING GROUP

SPARKS CENTENNIAL COMMISSION

SPARKS HERITAGE MUSEUM

WASHOE COUNTY LIBRARY

Table of Contents

Above: Dick Graves' Nugget. (1955)

50 Years

RENO/SPARKS LARGEST CASINO, RESTAURANT, HOTEL, ENTERTAINMENT and CONVENTION CENTER

For more than half a century, John Ascuaga and Northern Nevada have been inextricably linked. In fact, the great growth and evolution of John Ascuaga's Nugget Casino-Resort — originally a 60-seat coffee shop with only a handful of slot machines — has been a mirror image of the region's explosive expansion. John Ascuaga's Nugget Casino-Resort has become an emblem of the great American success story of John Ascuaga and his family.

John Ascuaga was born in Caldwell, Idaho, in 1925. His father, Jose, a Basque sheepherder from Spain, came to America in 1914. Jose and his wife, Marina, had four children, including John. From his father, young John learned the value of hard work and education. Following graduation from college — John earned a degree in accounting from the University of Idaho in 1951 and a degree in hotel and restaurant management from Washington State

Above: Sparks Mayor Seth Burgess honors Dick Graves and John Ascuaga with a key to the City of Sparks on opening day of the Nugget, March 17, 1955, at 11 a.m.

Right: Postcard of the Nugget. (1962)

University in 1952 — Ascuaga met another important figure in his life: restaurateur Dick Graves. Ascuaga became food manager for Graves' Idaho properties, and in 1954 he was named food director for Graves' Nevada restaurants. Ascuaga's duties included managing a small café-casino called Dick Graves' Nugget, which opened in northern Nevada on Saint Patrick's Day, March 17, 1955. Its location was right across from the current casino-resort's address on B Street in Sparks.

With Graves' retirement in 1960, Ascuaga purchased the Nugget and became sole owner and operator. Ascuaga's work ethic, already formidable, became the stuff of legend over the next several decades. With a business style that has been described as "never-stand still," Ascuaga emphasized that everything must be done with care, quality and integrity.

Not surprisingly, he built the Nugget into one of Nevada's largest casino-hotel operations. Today, John Ascuaga's Nugget Casino-Resort features 1,600 hotel rooms, casino areas totaling 75,000 square feet, convention facilities with more than 110,000 square feet, eight award-winning restaurants, a race and sports book, keno areas, a bingo parlor, a poker parlor, a unique indoor/outdoor swimming pool, a wedding chapel, an exercise area, a salon and spa, a video arcade, a cabaret, a

Nevada State Journal

NUGGET

SOUVENIR SUPPLEMENT, CARSON CITY AND SPARKS, NEVADA

ADVERTISEMENT

Nugget Causes Business Boom

Graves' New Casino-restaurant Welcome Adjunct to Sparks Life

There are business people in Sparks today, oldtimers included, who would want you to believe that the biggest boon to Sparks economy since the advent of the Southern Pacific, is a solid looking, tastefully decorated gambling establishment and cafe called the Nugget, which opened its doors on St. Patrick's Day, March 17.

To the guilding light and owner of the business, 6' 5" Richard L. (Dick) Graves, the reception his establishment has received from the people of Sparks has left him speechless—almost.

Graves, 42, a veteran of 20 years in the business, has good promotional ideas about his type of operation and even at this early date bodes well of becoming a legend in Sparks business life, or at best a real shot in the arm for activity on "B" street.

No sooner had he opened the doors for his $200,000 Nugget, than Graves, with no desire for recognition, immediately pledged his resources in full support of an advertising campaign that Sparks merchants have been advocating for years—"Shop and Save in Sparks." He has purchased hundreds of ads on all mediums promoting Sparks Friday night shopping.

Fully realizing that people in Nevada are going to patronize casinos, regardless, Graves feels the best thing to do is make them as comfortable as possible and give them something for their money. At the Sparks Nugget he has spared no expense to do either. Included are a $40,000 heating and air conditioning plant, a terrazzo floor that costs $1.50 a square foot and the best of facilities throughout.

Quiet, unassuming and highly successful in his past operations, (he owned six restaurants at one time) Graves many years ago met a man in Idaho who has furnished him with the key to the success he has enjoyed. The grizzled veteran, Jake Carruthers, said to Graves, "Dick, you're just getting started. Always remember you'll make all the money you can ever use if you heed this one thought—ya gotta send out winners to get players"...

Graves says he never could understand why a city the size of Sparks, (third or fourth largest in the state) did not have a first class casino and cafe. This, then, is the culmination of a hunch and as he stood there with a house full of patrons, Graves stated "maybe the hunch was right."

Like many another prominent gaming operator, Graves followed the trail to Nevada, feeling that the ultimate growth of the state and a sound economy found here, plus the unlimited opportunities offered, would be a good place in which he could stake his "claim."

His Nugget at Carson has enjoyed phenomenal success and has grown from an establishment employing 35 persons to a high of 85 at the present time. He is now in the process of adding other facilities including a charcoal broiler dining room to be called the "Roundhouse" at Carson. Graves lives in Carson with his wife and four children, and 200 Carson residents were on hand at the opening of the Nugget at Sparks. Graves feels the same about Carson as he does about Sparks. He says both communities are just now ready to bust at the seams and blossom out into even more prosperous communities and sound business locations.

Graves speaks highly of merchants at Sparks and says he has received wholehearted support from businessmen there. A good many of them have come to his place of business, introduced themselves and have approved of his moving into their community.

In exchange for the reception he has received Graves says he has endeavored to hire as many Sparks people as possible. Of the 95 persons employed at the Sparks Nugget, Graves estimates that at least 40 of them are residents of Sparks. "This policy will continue," says the lanky Idahoan.

To cooperate with his associates along "B" street, Graves has instituted a coupon point system. The points can be used with most cooperating merchants, who then present the coupons to the Nugget and receive a check for the merchandise given to the customer.

Graves speaks highly of his key personnel at Sparks. His general manager is John Ascuaga, a former food concession man who has been elevated to general manager. John is a blur of a man, short in stature but a human dynamo. Three men, Bob Tillotson, Bill Carter and Ole Severson, are assistant managers, Ned Adams handles the casino, Joe Peroglio the keno. Al Sines is head chef for the 65 seat capacity restaurant.

What has impressed Graves more than anything is the reception he has received at Sparks. And, feeling as he does about Nevada, Graves plans to be here a long time.

A great believer in advertising, Graves has brought to Nevada that doughty, grub-staker, strictly fictional, "Last Chance Joe." The voice for Last Chance Joe, says Graves, is Don Allen, a 27-year-old radio announcer from station KLIX at Twin Falls, Idaho. And "Ol' Las Chance," expounds the theme of giving people something for their money, for, says the old prospector, "players have got to win or they won't play."

Graves also has ideas about building or remodeling. He says he wouldn't even build a chicken house without consulting an architect and he also puts in a recommendation for a young Reno building contractor, Allen Galla-way, who did the work on the Sparks Nugget. Architect on the project was Frank Green.

For persons who visit the Nugget, who can't figure out what the slogan above the restaurant means: in English it reads as follows: "Here Stop and Spend a Social Hour, in Harmless Mirth and Fun—Let Friendship Reign—Be Just and Kind—And Evil Speak of None."

And a man, who has been successful for these many years, with a solid investment to offer the people of Sparks, could well turn out to be—the biggest boon to the town's economy since the coming of the railroad.

Last Chance Joe sez: "You gotta send out winners to get players."

KEYS TO CITY—Old-time Sparks resident and the town's mayor, Seth Burgess, (center), left is John Ascuaga, manager of the Nugget, which includes a 65-person-capacity restaurant, as well as gaming facilities. (Ross photo).

Johnny Ascuaga Sparks Manager

Small, Bustling Man Trained in Job

Little JOHNNY ASCUAGA, who is small enough to hide in Dick Graves' vest pocket but lively enough to set a whole town rocking, is the general manager of the Nugget in Sparks.

At 30, Johnny is described by Mr. Graves as the youngest man ever to have the responsibility of managing an operation of the Nugget's scope.

Johnny claims to be a "confirmed" batchelor. He grew up on a farm in Caldwell, Idaho, and served with the Army of Occupation in Japan following World War II. Four years ago he joined Mr. Graves' staff as a restaurant manager in Coeur D'Alene, Idaho.

JOHN ASCUAGA

Restaurants and clubs are Johnny's whole life, and he loves them. He settled on his career after working five summers as a bellboy at an Idaho resort hotel.

For professional training, John attended Washington State College, where he majored in restaurant and hotel management, and the University of Idaho, where he majored in accounting.

Chances are you won't get too good a look at Johnny when you visit the Nugget, because he doesn't stand still long enough.

Businessmen Praise Nugget's Operation

Friday Night Shopping Plan Grows As Trade Drawn to Sparks Area

In Sparks, Nugget owner Dick Graves has proved the adage that success builds success.

For, in building up his Nugget into Sparks' liveliest business, he has helped almost every other businessman achieve greater prosperity.

With the Nugget drawing more trade into the community than Sparks has seen for many years, the Sparks Chamber of Commerce and almost 100 per cent of the B St. business houses have expanded their Friday night shopping program from a monthly to a weekly event.

Virtually every business house in Sparks is open every Friday night until 9 p.m. and, thanks in part to the attraction of the Nugget, there is an abundance of customers.

Dick Graves profits by this, too, for when the stores close, many of the shoppers gravitate to his casino and 24-hour restaurant before going home.

The Nugget encourages the Friday night trade for the whole community by extensive advertising. At no expense to the shop owners, it has printed large placards boosting Friday night shopping and has distributed them to all shopkeepers for display. The placards don't have a solitary word of Nugget advertising on them.

Buster Brannin, owner of Brannin's Sparks Radio Service, is one of the storekeepers who has found his own business booming right along with the Nugget's.

"The Nugget has helped me a lot so far, and I know it will help me in the future," says the jovial Mr. Brannin. "I have been in Sparks a long time, but it is only since the Nugget opened that I have seen both sides of B St. filled up with parkers during the middle-of-the-week evenings."

One of the first supporters of Friday night shopping in Sparks, Mr. Brannin feels that the Nugget has helped draw a lot of customers to town for evening shopping through promotional advertising and other means.

Carl Shelly, publisher of the Sparks Tribune and owner of the Modern Home Mart hardware store on B St., is another Nugget booster.

"The Nugget has helped my business a lot," Mr. Shelly said. "It has created a great deal of foot traffic in the business district, which is helpful to all of our businesses."

At first thought it would seem unlikely, but the Nugget has also helped business far removed from the B St. shopping area. One of the businesses which got a boost when the Nugget opened was the Sparks Frozen Food Lockers at 1436 Prater Way, an enterprise not directly affected by the increased number of people on B St.

Says owner E. J. Iratcabal, "Of course the Nugget has helped our business, just as it has helped business throughout Sparks.

Graves Starts College Fund

Plans to perpetuate the scholarship plan launched ten years ago by Harold's Club have been proposed by Nugget owner Dick Graves.

Harold's Club, largest casino in Nevada, had to drop the million-dollar University of Nevada scholarship plan for financial reasons late in April.

Graves said he would take up the two yearly $4,000 scholarships for Sparks and Carson City, where his businesses are located. He expressed hope that other casino owners throughout the state would voluntarily provide for the remaining 28 scholarships ordinarily offered each year by Harold's Club.

"Harold's Club founded a fine institution," Graves said. "The financial burden is too much for one club to carry, however. I am in hopes all the clubs will chip in to keep the scholarships going permanently."

Above: A special six-page advertising section in the Nevada State Journal chronicles the progress of Dick Graves and John Ascuaga with the Nugget. (1955)

'What's Fair Is Fair'

ght on Target
or Accuracy

aper Work
educed

Above: The Nugget's 30th anniversary is covered in the "Nugget Scene," the Nugget's quarterly publication for employees. George Wilkes, bakery manager, and Susan Shepherd, head decorator, spent five days preparing the cake for display in the hotel lobby during the celebration. At the time the cake was the most massive ever to come from the Nugget bakery. (1985)

1,900-seat concert area, the Celebrity Showroom and Business Center.

John Ascuaga resides on his 1,250-acre Jack's Valley Ranch in northern Douglas County. The Ascuaga Cattle Company for years supplied a large amount of beef to the Nugget and featured some of the finest purebred Herefords in the West. In tribute to his father and in homage to the Basque sheepherding tradition, Ascuaga still keeps a flock of sheep at Jack's Valley Ranch.

Known for his approach to business and his ability to relate in a meaningful way to people in all walks of life, Ascuaga is in great demand throughout northern Nevada as a speaker, member of prominent boards and as a philanthropist. The community remains one of Ascuaga's great causes. His efforts in this area have included providing $500,000 to date in annual scholarships to northern Nevada high school students, Thanksgiving and Christmas dinners to the homeless and needy at St. Vincent's Dining Room every year, ballroom and convention sites for programs that raise money for education, university sports programs and much more.

He is also a supporter of the Basque community and culture. In an interview with the Basque Studies Program at the University of Nevada, Reno, Ascuaga noted that he was proud of his Basque heritage: "Basque people are not sheepherders anymore. ... But many of them are now very successful business people." And at the front of this new generation of successful Basque business people is a man who has helped mold northern Nevada's image into its successfully modern form: John Ascuaga.

Timeline

March 17, 1955

The Nugget opens in Sparks on the north side of B Street. It's a 60-seat coffee shop with about 50 slot machines.

August 4, 1955

"Happy" Bill Howard, who two years earlier had set the world pole-sitting record of 196 days, takes his perch on a 6-foot-wide platform 60 feet above the Nugget parking lot. It's the most outrageous promotion to date by publicity-minded owner Dick Graves. A long-bearded Howard comes down 204 days later, pocketing $6,800.

May 13, 1958

Nugget moves to the south side of B Street. Doors close on the old property, patrons move into the middle of the street and keep right on gambling, then doors open on the new property — a 36,000-square-foot casino, five restaurants, two bars and banquet rooms.

December 1958

U.S. Treasury officials inform Graves that the 15-pound, solid-gold rooster he had commissioned to stand outside one of the restaurants violates the 1934 Gold Reserve Act. After four years of legal wrangling, including federal confiscation of the statuette, a jury decides in the Nugget's favor and the rooster is returned home.

December 13, 1958

Trader Dick's restaurant opens at the northeast corner of B and 12th streets. Trader Dick's moved to the present Nugget building Feb. 9, 1973, then to its current location on Feb. 16, 1988.

October 1, 1960

Graves, longing to retire, sells the Nugget's operating company to his 34-year-old manager, John Ascuaga, for $3.775 million and nothing down. Terms call for paying it off in 12 years. Ascuaga manages the feat in seven.

Nugget Observes 25th Anniversary

NUGGET GAZETTE — *John Ascuaga's NUGGET*

JOHN ASCUAGA'S NUGGET - P.O. BOX 797, SPARKS, NEVADA

NUGGET OPENS $1½ MILLION ADDITION

24,000 SQUARE FEET FEATURES CABARET, ENLARGED DINING, COCKTAIL, BANQUET AND CASINO AREAS!

Left: The Nugget opens its $1.5 million expansion on June 13, 1974, which added more slots for a total of 1,100 machines.

Top: John Ascuaga's Nugget celebrated its 25th Anniversary with an elaborate party including cake and coffee for every guest. (1980)

Above: The Nugget celebrates its 35th anniversary. (1990)

Above: The Golden Rooster sits proudly in the hotel lobby of John Ascuaga's Nugget. (2004)

Right: Dick Graves and John Ascuaga with the specially commissioned, 15-pound, "Golden Rooster." (1958)

Below Right: John Ascuaga places the infamous Golden Rooster in its specially made case that is now proudly displayed in the hotel lobby. (1988)

The Story of the Nugget's
Gold Rooster

It was May 1958. The Nugget was preparing to open a new restaurant—the Golden Rooster Room. But one question remained unanswered: what could be done to give specific identity to the new facility. The Nugget's other dining rooms had their own insignia, themes and menus—and so should it be for the Golden Rooster Room.

Management scheduled a "think tank" session and an idea was soon born: make a solid gold statue of a rooster, regal and beautiful—one that could be classified as a masterpiece of art, one that could be displayed and admired by all Nugget guests.

Permission was quickly granted by the San Francisco Mint to make the Golden Rooster. Newman's Silver Shop of Reno and Shreve's of San Francisco were commissioned to fashion the objet d'art from a model created by sculptor-artist Frank Polk.

Within four months the 18-karat gold statue was completed, transported under guard to Reno, and placed in a custom-made glass case near the entrance to the Golden Rooster Room. The beauty of the sculpture, the uniqueness of the work, its value as precious metal—all combined to give the Rooster immediate status as a "must see" attraction for local residents as well as tourists.

Seven months after being on exhibit, the Golden Rooster attracted the attention of the United States Treasury Department, with officials charging that the Nugget was in violation of the Gold Reserve Act which makes it unlawful for a private individual to have more than 50 ounces of gold in his possession unless it is in the form of an object of art.

The Rooster would have to be confiscated.

The Nugget pleaded its case, informing Treasury representatives that permission had been granted through Shreve's by the U.S. Mint. Following verification of the facts by the Treasury, the matter was dropped—for 18 months.

In July 1960 the Nugget was again visited by officers of the Treasury—this time to present the Nugget with a complaint entitled "United States of America vs. One Solid Gold Object in the Form of a Rooster." The Rooster was confiscated and would have to go to jail. The Nugget's attempt to "put up bail" was denied.

After "serving" two years, and after two trial postponements, the Golden Rooster was to have his day in court. The decision would center on one question: was the Golden Rooster an object of art. The Nugget contended the Rooster was a customary and artistic use of gold. The Government disagreed.

At a jury trial in March 1962 the Government was unable to sway the testimony of art critics—all of whom agreed with the Nugget. And so did the jury of ten men and two women.

The Golden Rooster was freed.

And newspapers and wire services throughout the nation carried the story. News headlines shouted: "Solid Gold Bird Liberated."

Amid much display of public approval, the Golden Rooster was returned to the Nugget and its special perch at the entrance to the Golden Rooster Room.

In 1987, when workmen began dismantling the Golden Rooster Room to provide space for a new and enlarged Trader Dick's Restaurant and Lounge, the Rooster was again placed "under wraps" in a secured vault to await another decision: where best could it be returned for public display.

With the completion of the Nugget's new hotel lobby and convention center, the answer was obvious.

In its new and present location in the hotel lobby, the Golden Rooster is readily visible to all Nugget guests—and again the gold statue is the center of attention.

GOLDEN ROOSTER VITAL STATISTICS

Artistic Value Appraisal in October 1988: $61,784
Height: 9.5 inches
Weight: 206.3 troy ounces (14.1 avoirdupois pounds)
Insured for $140,000
18-Karat Solid Gold

TB-3561-08/89-10M

October 20, 1960
Nugget Motor Lodge opens

June 21, 1962
Circus Room opens with "The International Follies," featuring a comic, a singer, a banjoist and a chorus line. Entertainment soon included such headliners as Jimmy Durante, Dinah Shore and Liberace. Debuting with the room's opening is an 11-year-old elephant bought on a whim from a circus in Baraboo, Wis. Bertha's status grows and grows until she's the de facto mascot for the Nugget and Sparks.

July 1962
The Roof Garden Hotel opens.

1964
The Nugget Inn opens.

August 1965
The Convention Center opens on the north side of B Street, east of Security Pacific Bank, which has long since been demolished.

June 1972
Ascuaga completes purchase of Graves' remaining downtown Sparks land holdings.

1972
What is now the Trader Dick's area and the area occupied by cashiers and credit (former Bingo section) opens.

June 13, 1974
The Casino Cabaret opens.

1976
The Nugget Meat Plant opens, providing meat for not only the Nugget but other casinos and restaurants in northern Nevada.

April 28, 1978
The General Store Restaurant and additional casino space opens.

September 10, 1979
The Convention Center on the second and third floors (pre-hotel tower) opens.

September 19, 1983
Groundbreaking for the first hotel tower.

June 19, 1984
The Rotisserie Buffet opens.

December 26, 1984
The 610-room hotel tower opens, making the Nugget the rival of the large Reno hotel-casinos. Ascuaga has steadily plowed profits back into the property, resulting in seven restaurants and a large casino area.

June-July 1985
The lower-level Pavilion with the Bingo Parlor, Poker Room, Race & Sports Book, Pub & Pantry and Gift Shop opens.

September 12, 1988
The $20 million construction begins on a three-floor addition with a pool and spa, hotel lobby and the Rose Ballroom/convention center. All are opened by January 1990. In August 1991, the fifth-floor Poolside Terrace opens.

August 1, 1989
Hotel Lobby and Convention Center (Ballroom) open. The 80,000 square foot area makes the Nugget a major convention destination.

September 1989
The Sports Book opens next to the Race Book.

January 17, 1990
Indoor-outdoor Atrium Pool opens.

August 1990
Newly remodeled Motor Lodge opens as the Courtyard, and includes a wedding chapel.

December 17, 1990
Chonne's Beauty Salon and Spa opens.

Left: A towering birthday cake is prepared by Eric Prime and Janet Whitaker for the Nugget's 35th anniversary. It was 12-feet high, contained 25 tiers, weighed 500 pounds with 300 pounds of icing, took 20 man-hours to prepare and had 1,500 roses. (1990) *Photo by Marilyn Newton*

Below: When the Nugget's first tower opened in December 1984, Red Skelton helped celebrate this important event with a special performance.

Above: Dick Graves' Nugget, with Last Chance Joe. (1958)

Right: Wrecking crews on April 24, 1992, tore down the former Gold Club casino on Victorian Square. John Ascuaga's Nugget purchased the facility, which had employed 26 people before closing in 1991. It sat between the Nugget and the Nugget Motor Lodge. *Photo by Marilyn Newton.*

Below Right: In 2004 John Ascuaga's Nugget features 110,000 square feet of convention space. The Nugget is the second largest convention hotel in northern Nevada and hosts conventions and trade shows from around the country.

February 13, 1991
Newly remodeled Steakhouse Grill opens.

August 1991
Poolside Terrace on fifth floor opens.

November 1991
New Card Room opens in Pavilion north of Bingo.

December 1991
Newly remodeled Gift Shop opens.

April 1992
Gold Club is purchased and the building is demolished.

September 1992
The warehouse is completed at 350 Edison Way.

October 15, 1992
A $1 million state-of-the-art neon sign over the west parking lot is lighted, flashing messages to Interstate 80 traffic.

November 1992
Nugget Avenue extension is complete from the Interstate 80 exit to Pyramid Way.

December 1993
Total renovation of tower hotel rooms is completed.

March and April 1994
The Race and Sportsbook area is expanded to accommodate more guests. At the same time, Gabe's Pub and Deli opens serving breakfast, lunch and dinner.

April 1994
Club Level accommodations open in hotel tower. Upgrades include televisions in bathrooms, nightly turndown service, coffee makers and higher-grade security.

May 1994
New high-tech laundry facility opens to accommodate the Nugget's 4 million pounds of wash each year. New loading dock also is completed.

Bomb scare shuts Nugget

- **6,000 evacuated:** 7 square blocks of Sparks a ghost town
- **Device found:** Officials X-ray box chained to column
- **Could take days:** Police proceed cautiously, close I-80

By Mike Henderson
GAZETTE-JOURNAL

Experts were carefully examining a suspected bomb early today after an alleged extortionist Friday told an official of John Ascuaga's Nugget an explosive device had been placed in the casino.

The 1,000-room hotel-casino and block surrounding ar... p.m. As many as 6,00... by residents and all gu... get and nearby hotels... minutes.

By early this mornin... were allowed to return.

The Nugget's operat... phone call about 9:30 a... son who informed him... in the casino, said Rick... counsel.

Sparks police and the... cated the box, he said.

It was still unclear thi... more than five-hour dela... and evacuating the hotel-... son said evacuation wasn... so advised Ascuaga.

Both lanes of Interstate... parts of the Nugget — wer... enue exit in Reno to McCa... There was no estimate as to...

Early today, officials we... raying and using fiber opt... num box on wheels roughl... desk-top photocopier, Dave...

Officials could not confir... an iron column in a constr... lobby, contained a bomb an...

Officials searched for a se... tionary measure but did not f...

A bomb-sniffing dog and... arrived in Reno today to su... and the FBI, said Steve Mu... spokesman.

If the device is indeed a... said, it could be as much as s... removed and normal busines... first X-rays provided by equip... Douglas County Sheriff's Depa... sive and authorities were takin...

Davenport and Sparks polic... fused to say whether the alleg... money or something else and r... the caller was male or female.

At a 4 p.m. news conference, S... been no contact with the extorti... At an 8 p.m. news conference h... when asked if there had been anot...

There was no estimate of how... amination would take.

"If it takes (days), then we will... ville said. "We'll do what it take... there and be cowboys and heroes... thing happen"

The hotel-casino was nearly full for the Great Reno Balloon Race weekend. Police closed Interstate 80 at 3 p.m. and scores of fire, police, ambulance, Salvation Army, Red Cross and other rescue personnel were poised for action within a few blocks of the

See **BOMB** on page **5A**

GHOST TOWN: All is eerily quiet on I-80 and in Victorian Square in the neighborhood of the Nugget Friday. *Marilyn Newton/Gazette-Journal*

More inside
Traffic trouble: Tourists, residents flee Nugget neighborhood, turning area into sea of confusion. **6A**

Deja vu: Nugget extortion plot similar to 1980 Harvey's bomb plot. **6A**

Economic impact: Closings could cost casinos at least $2 million each day; mini-marts prosper. **7A**

Displaced: Stranded hotel guests end up at convention center. **7A**

MOVE ALONG: A Sparks police officer Friday tells people they can't hang around near John Ascuaga's Nugget on Victorian Avenue in Sparks. The 1,000-room hotel-casino and seven-square-block surrounding area were evacuated starting at 3 p.m. As many as 6,000 people were evacuated in about 90 minutes after a bomb threat was received. *Craig Sailor/Gazette-Journal*

HOTLINE
LATEST INFORMATION
■ **What's the latest news concerning the Nugget extortion case?** Call **324-0225**, then press **6397**. The Gazette-Journal will update the news as the situation changes.

Nugget back in action

3 full pages of coverage inside, 11-13A

- **Bomb scare ends safely:** Hundreds return after shutdown of downtown Sparks.
- **Hunt on:** Police seek extortionist.

By Courtney Brenn
GAZETTE-JOURNAL

John Ascuaga's Nugget reopened Saturday after bomb experts removed a large metal box that didn't contain any explosive material.

The hoax was revealed after a tense, 24-hour examination of the device by more than 65 bomb experts from around the country.

The box is being sent to Washington, D.C., to be combed over by FBI forensic experts as federal and local officials step up their search for whoever planted the box behind a temporary wall in the south lobby of the 1,000-room hotel.

Although details remained sketchy late Saturday, the 3-by-3-by-4-foot box was apparently part of an extortion attempt against the Nugget.

An anonymous caller contacted the casino by phone at 9:30 Friday morning and warned of a bomb. Officials found the device where the caller said it would be, and 5½ hours later the hotel and surrounding businesses were evacuated around the Ascuaga

Officials will not say if there have been any other contacts with extortionists, or if there were any demands. They said they are pursuing a number of investigative leads in the case, and that they believe the box was planted sometime between midnight and 9:30 a.m. Friday.

The metal box, found chained to an iron column in a construction area, was trucked to a remote desert area off Vista Boulevard shortly after 11 a.m. Saturday. Bomb crews were seen hiding behind their vehicles while a small, remote-controlled blast went off on top of the box. Investigators then gathered around it to look inside.

Federal Bureau of Investigation agent Burk Smith said danger to the town ended after bomb spe-

See **NUGGET** on page **11A**

OPENING DEVICE: Bomb experts blow lid off of box removed from Nugget on Saturday. *Craig Sailor/Gazette-Journal*

GUESTS: Edna Sanford and Viola Hill, both of Red Bluff, Calif., head home after getting their belongings after the Nugget reopened on Saturday. *Tim Dunn/Gazette-Journal*

More inside:
- **"Money doesn't mean anything when your building's still intact and your employees are going back to work."** — John Ascuaga
  Interview with hotel owner after tense 27 hours. **12A**
- **Unharmed again:** This wasn't first hardship Ascuaga overcame. **12A**
- **Extortion anatomy:** Graphic depiction of the two-day ordeal. **11A**
- **No second chances:** High stakes for bomb experts. **11A**
- **Back to life:** Gambler wins $18,000 just after casino reopens. **13A**
- **Plus photos, more**

FINANCIAL IMPACT

Casinos may lose $2 million a day

■ **Nugget hit the worst:** Affect on victim of extortion attempt likely to be substantial.

By Wayne R. Melton
GAZETTE-JOURNAL

Downtown Sparks casinos will lose a combined estimated $2 million in gross revenues for every 24-hour period they're closed, a noted gaming industry analyst said.

And Friday's crisis couldn't have come at a worse time of year for the Truckee Meadows' gaming industry, since this period historically marks the start of the region's busiest one-week period for tourism, he said.

September is typically the region's biggest tourism month, with events like this weekend's Great Reno Balloon Race and next weekend's Reno National Championship Air races.

These events bring tens of thousands of visitors to the Truckee Meadows. Many of them stay in local hotels and gamble in casinos.

There was still no word on how ... y potential visitors, if any, ... led plans to visit Reno and ... ks this weekend as a result of ... risis. Much will depend on ... er the situation is resolved, ... officials said.

... would hope it wouldn't have ... verse impact" on the number ... tors, said Carol Infranca, ... unications chief for the ... Sparks Convention & Visi... uthority.

... Friday evening, there still ... least 500 available hotel ... at Truckee Meadows facili... ... directly impacted by the ... , she said.

... biggest loss will be at John ... 's Nugget, the victim of an ... on attempt, gaming offi... d.

... ublic safety reasons, police ... ed the Silver Club, The ... Club, the Mint and Carl ... B Street Gambling Hall. ... sure hurt them (all) in ... revenue," said the consul... o asked that his name not ... "The Nugget is by far the

... sses to privately owned ... not a matter of public re... ... they would be substan... Nugget has 73,900 square ... asino floorspace, second ... the 100,000-square-foot ... on in the Truckee Mead...

... s and competitors in re... have described the Nug... ong the nation's best ... — and perhaps one of ... rofitable — large casi...

... analysts and gaming ... estimate that after ... mary operations ex... ,950-room Nugget gen... verage $60 million in ... nnual revenue.

... nationally known gam... expert, William Ead... t would be "flippant" ... the economic impact ... get, or on the entire ... t the start of the cri...

... want to sound crass, ... more than the eco... ct involved," said ... director of the Insti-

NUGGET HOTEL OFFICIALS
■ **Owner:** John Ascuaga Trust
■ **Chief executive:** Tonnis "Tony" Lubbers
■ **Operations chief:** Mack Potter

tute for the Study of Gambling and Commercial Gaming at the University of Nevada, Reno.

It also would be premature to predict how much, if at all, widespread news of the event might cut down on tourism this weekend and throughout the coming week, he said.

With these factors in mind, Eadington said, the closures affect the casinos just as shutdowns would affect businesses in almost any industry.

"It's down time, clearly like having a 747 aircraft down for general maintenance and repair," he said. "For the period properties are closed, they lose revenues."

Thus, the eventual economic loss to the casinos will depend in large part on the amount of time they're closed, he said. In addition, depending on the outcome of the situation, there may be re-start costs involved.

It's also likely some families will suffer an economic loss because of cases where employees aren't paid due to the casino closures, he said.

However, Eadington emphasized that each crisis is different. He said the Harvey's Resort extortion attempt and bombing in the early 1980s is the only similar case that can be reviewed for comparison purposes.

Although Harvey's was destroyed, that crisis didn't have any strong overall negative short- and long-term impacts on that region's tourism and gaming economy, Eadington said.

Gary Royer, owner of the Casino Control Consulting firm in Reno, said he's surprised the extortionist chose the Nugget since it's owned by a family, rather than a huge corporation.

Casinos that are operated by large firms have far more assets to potentially lose than would a single family, Royer said.

For this reason, "I would think it would be the last operation anybody would put a bomb in," he said. "It would seem to me that an expert would try to do it with a large, publicly traded corporation."

Authorities stressed that the crisis was in a specific business district, and that the remainder of the Truckee Meadows gaming industry remained open for business.

However, when "you're talking about something that might indirectly impact events like the air races or the balloon races, this could have a huge ripple effect throughout our economy," he said. "It'll depend on what happens."

Left & Above: In September 1993 the Nugget was evacuated due to a bomb scare. This is a photo of the device that was found. While it was eventually discovered to be a fake, the entire area was evacuated.

Right: The Bingo parlor. (1999)

Below: Artist's rendering of the Nugget's neon sign that overlooks I-80. (1992)

September 2, 1994
The $9 million, five-story parking garage with 1,252 vehicle spaces opens. It has
security lighting and a skyway above 11th Street to the second floor.

December 1994
The Skywalk Video Arcade opens on the second floor of the Convention Center.

March 17, 1995
The Nugget celebrates its 40th anniversary. The Nugget is now a 958-room hotel with a 75,000-square-foot casino, an 80,000-square-foot convention center and eight restaurants.

November 29, 1995
Groundbreaking for the second Hotel Tower.

December 26, 1996
802-room West Tower opens with 30,000 square feet more of convention space and 100 suites. Making the Nugget one of the largest convention hotels in the region.

October 1997
Michonne Ascuaga is named chief executive officer for John Ascuaga's Nugget.

August 11, 1998
Restaurante Orozko, named for the Basque village in northern Spain from which John Ascuaga's father emigrated, opens.

October 1999
Seven grand suites, built at a cost of $2 million, open. They are reserved for special guests.

November 9, 1999
Bertha passes away at age 48. Shortly after Bertha's death, Angel is moved to an elephant sanctuary at the Fort Worth Zoo.

August 1, 2002
Newly remodeled Rosie's Café opens replacing the General Store.

February 25, 2003
The Nugget Meat Packers closed after providing packaged beef and pork for commercial and personal sales in northern Nevada since 1976.

March 18, 2004
The Nugget Convention Center reopened after a $1 million renovation that included new carpet, new wallpaper, paint, lighting fixtures and the latest in T1 technology — allowing high-speed Internet access with fiber-optic connectivity.

Above: He stepped off the boat from Holland in 1957 as a pastry chef. Forty years later Tonnis Lubbers, a dapper executive with a penchant for storytelling, stepped down as chief executive officer of John Ascuaga's Nugget in a career full of accomplishments. He joined the Nugget in 1962 as banquet manager, and climbed the management ladder until being named CEO in 1985. Food, meanwhile, was Lubbers' first love, and it shows in the attention to detail in the Nugget's restaurants that continues today. And Lubbers called completion of the Nugget's first hotel tower in December 1984 among the most memorable moments in his career. Big, too, was the opening of the second tower in December 1996, for which he postponed his retirement. *Photo by Jean Dixon*

Right: Cor Van der Stokker, left, Yves Lesquereux and Tonnis Lubbers represent over 120 years of combined food, hospitality and service experience. Cor, Yves and Tonnis were all instrumental in making John Ascuaga's Nugget food and service legendary. (1997)

The Nugget

Above: During the move from the north side of B Street, liquor had to be carried over by hand. (1958)

Above Right: John Ascuaga mans the gears in the 1961 groundbreaking of the Nugget expansion, which was completed in 1962.

Opposite: Emmett Kelly brought his ever-present broom to help John Ascuaga with the groundbreaking for the 1961 expansion of the Nugget.

It was once a small casino with a handful of slot machines and a 60-seat café. But in every decade since its opening in 1955, John Ascuaga's Nugget has transformed, reinventing itself into Sparks' grandest casino-resort. With its first location on the north side of then B Street — now Victorian Avenue — the Nugget was a locals' favorite, a hangout with good food and a few games to pass the time. But owing to its owner's vision for the future, expansion was always in the game plan.

A mere three years after its opening, the Nugget crossed B Street with an expanded casino and a new dining favorite — Trader Dick's. Then came the early '60s, when the focus shifted to include lodging. The years 1960 through 1964 saw the opening of the Motor Lodge, the Roof Garden Hotel and the Nugget Inn.

With expansion happening in every direction, meeting space now was on the menu. In August 1965, the Nugget opened the doors to its original Convention Center — most likely with little knowledge that future convention space would comprise 110,000 square feet. Incrementally the Nugget expanded, steadily adding to its casino floor throughout the '70s.

The property broke ground on its first tower in late 1983. On Dec. 26, 1984, Sparks residents awoke to a late Christmas present — the "new exclamation point in the sky," as then-Mayor Jim Spoo called it. The $44 million tower boasted 29 stories, 610 rooms, expanded convention and casino space and two new restaurants.

But the Nugget's master plan was far from complete, as 1990 saw the opening of the popular indoor/outdoor pool and health club. Then the final punctuation mark to adorn Sparks' skyline: a $70 million, 29-story second tower with a new restaurant, 30,000 square feet of additional convention space and 802

new hotel rooms.

A glance at the big picture reveals a graceful evolution, a 60-seat café transforming over the course of six decades into a 1,600-room casino resort with more than 75,000 square feet of casino space housing much more than a handful of slots — and more than even the greatest visionary could predict.

Top: John Ascuaga, right, shows new plans to Sparks City Manager Bob Rankin, left, Dick Graves and Sparks Mayor Ed Richards, in 1957, with regards to expanding the Nugget.

Above: It was moving day in May 1958. Everything was moved at night from the north side of B Street to the new Nugget on the south side. Here's a blackjack table.

Right: John Ascuaga himself pitched in with the night-time move, seen here lugging money with John Sheehan, left, and George Vucanovich.

This Photo: Slot machines are installed in preparation for eager guests. (1958)

Below: John Ascuaga and Sparks City Councilman Val Galleron at the opening of the Nugget Motor Lodge on Oct. 20, 1960.

Bottom Right: Dignitaries gather for the grand opening of Trader Dick's in November 1958, including John Ascuaga, front, and Dick Graves (behind Ascuaga). Trader Dick's Polynesian menu was considered innovative and exotic in the late 50s. Today, Trader Dick's is still known for delicious Asian-inspired dishes and tropical libations.

Right: Customers fill the newly opened casino. (1958)

Above: Completion nears for the Nugget Roof Garden Roomettes in 1962. The individual roomettes were 9 feet by 10 feet in size. Each featured a telephone, fold-down writing desk, heat and air, a bathroom with shower and storage area. Room rates at the time were $5 for a single and $7 for a double.

Right: John Ascuaga at the opening of the Nugget Motor Lodge on Oct. 20, 1960.

NEVADA STATE JOURNAL, RENO, NEVADA

DISJOINTED ARRIVAL

"Last Chance Joe" arrives from Los Angeles via Southern Pacific flatcar. The figure was shipped in three sections.
(Ross photo)

ARRIVAL AT JOINT

Economy Size Statue Here

A 35-foot high replica of "Last Chance Joe" was installed Monday on the front of Dick Graves' new million dollar Nugget casino in Sparks.

The figure is the largest ever built by the R. H. Grosh Scenic Studios of Los Angeles, creators of such famous Disneyland figures as Alice in Wonderland and Peter Pan. The company just recently finished a miniature replica of the Grand Canyon 32 feet high and 332 feet wide to be used in a new Disneyland addition.

"Last Chance Joe" was over three months in the making. It stands 35 feet high, is 15 feet wide (through the hat) eight feet thick and weighs slightly over 5,000 pounds.

As many as 20 Scenic Studio craftsmen worked on the figure at one time. Structural angle iron was used to frame the figure and then chicken wire was placed over the entire figure. Next, layer after layer of papier-mache was added and then two layers of a special glass cloth called celastic was applied. Finally, the figure was completely painted in full color and a plastic spray was added.

The "Last Chance Joe" was built and shipped in three sections via a single Southern Pacific flatcar. Workmen will seal and paint the joints where the figure goes together.

The new Nugget is scheduled to open around the middle of May and will include three restaurants, a chicken house, steak house, coffee shop and a banquet room.

A Reno Iron Works crane lowers the final section of "Last Chance Joe" into place on the front of the new Sparks Nugget. The man standing on top of the building allows good comparison for the size of the 35-foot-high figure.
(Ross photo)

Far Left: Last Chance Joe mascot at the Nugget used in advertising.

Near Left: A strange sight greeted people along the Southern Pacific Railroad's right of way in early 1958. From Los Angeles to Sparks, a papier-mache figure dubbed Tall Cowboy in news reports of the day could be seen on a flat car as it wound its way to Dick Graves' Nugget. It arrived in pieces, but when assembled and placed on the front of the Nugget it stood 32 feet high.

Above: Construction on the Nugget casino began in 1961.

Below: The expansion is complete and ready to open. (1962)

Opposite: A construction worker takes a gaming break during the Nugget expansion in 1961.

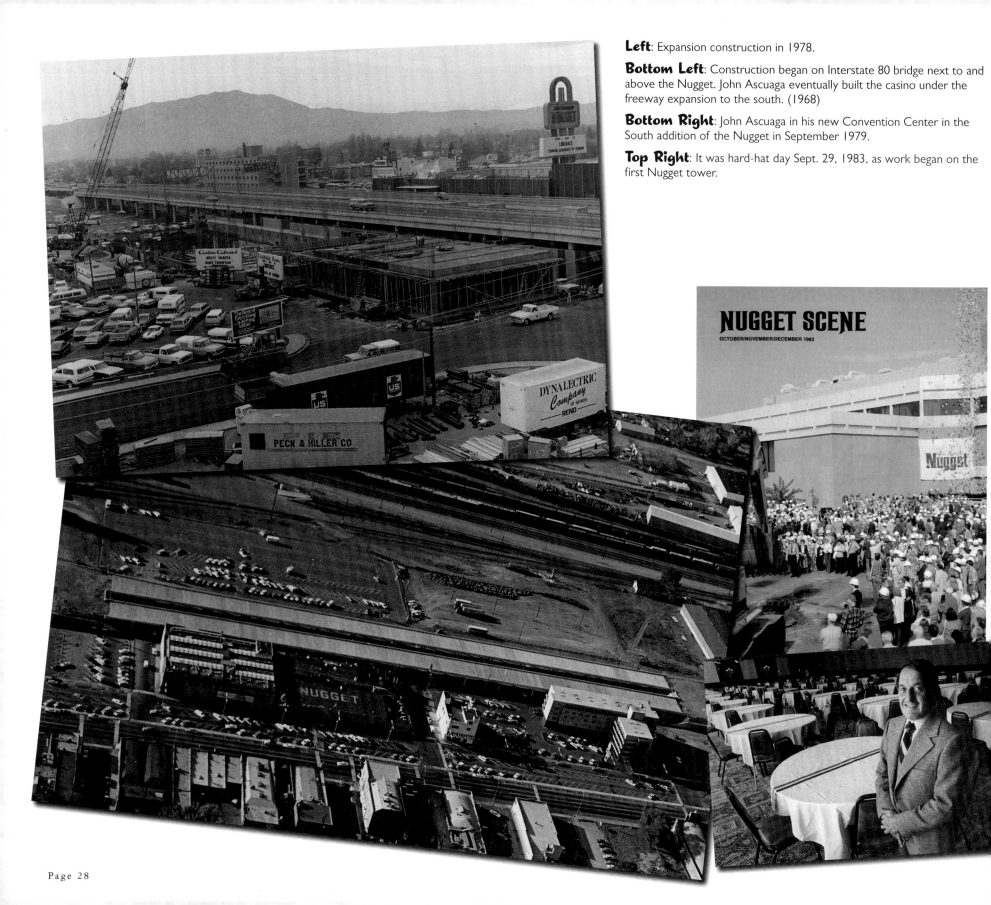

Left: Expansion construction in 1978.

Bottom Left: Construction began on Interstate 80 bridge next to and above the Nugget. John Ascuaga eventually built the casino under the freeway expansion to the south. (1968)

Bottom Right: John Ascuaga in his new Convention Center in the South addition of the Nugget in September 1979.

Top Right: It was hard-hat day Sept. 29, 1983, as work began on the first Nugget tower.

NUGGET SCENE

OCTOBER/NOVEMBER/DECEMBER 1983

Above: The Nugget tower two days before it opened the day after Christmas 1984. *Photo by James Flenner*

Right: Workmen position a Ponderosa pine during topping-off ceremonies Sept. 25, 1984, atop the new hotel tower. The tree came from John Ascuaga's Jack's Valley Ranch. *Photo by Marilyn Newton*

Above Left: The Nugget sign and two towers can be seen from the Eastbound lanes of Interstate 80. (1999) *Photo by Tim Dunn*

Left: The French Country suite is one of seven luxury rooms that opened in 1999. The suites cost about $2 million and are used by special guests. *Photo by Andy Barron*

Above: All seven of the exclusive suites have a theme and oversized amenities such as this tub in the Ascuaga suite.

Above: The Ascuaga Suite is one of the exclusive suites at the Nugget and features photos of John with celebrities and dignitaries. The suite also has a stunning view of the Sierra Nevada.

Right: The hotel lobby of John Ascuaga's Nugget. (1998)

This Photo: The Rose Ballroom can seat up to 2,000 people for dinner and concerts. (2004)

Below: The fifth floor swimming pool and spas opened in 1990. The Nugget was the first to feature an indoor/outdoor atrium pool.

Bottom Left: Inside a hotel room. (1998)

Bottom Right: Tahoe Suite

Middle Right: Chonne's Beauty Salon and Spa opened on Dec. 17, 1990, and is named after Michonne Ascuaga.

Right: The gift shop opened in June 1985 and features jewelry, clothes and special souvenirs.

Left: The Poolside Terrace is located on the fifth floor next door to the indoor/outdoor atrium pool and is a popular room for special dinners and wedding parties.

Bottom Left: A VIP Suite in the East Tower.

Bottom Right: The living room in the Tahoe Suite.

Below: The fifth floor indoor/outdoor atrium pool opened. (1990)

Opposite: The free parking garage at John Ascuaga's Nugget opened on Sept. 2, 1994, and features 1,252 guest parking spots.

Dining

From the beginning in 1955, John Ascuaga realized that giving people a great meal for a reasonable price would be his ticket to success. He insisted on quality, consistency and good service in the restaurants. In order to maintain the high culinary standards over the years, Ascuaga and his staff paid close attention to customers' comments. As the times and tastes changed, new restaurants opened and menus were updated frequently.

The original coffee shop, on the north side of B Street, was close to the busy railyard in Sparks. Accommodating just 60 people, it became a popular place for railroad workers as well as Reno-Sparks residents. The menu was short and simple, but full of hearty breakfast choices, steaks, stew, sandwiches and the famous Awful-Awful

Above: Jimmy Chan is the executive chef at John Ascuaga's Nugget in 2004. With 38 years food experience, Chan insures that the quality of food at the Nugget is still consistently high.

Right: Attendees take in dinner before a show in the Circus Room in 1963. The Circus Room featured two shows every night, with a dinner and cocktail performance.

This Photo: The new restaurant is all lit up for its grand opening in 1958. It would later move across the street inside the casino.

This Photo: The Awful Awful Girl was used to publicize the famous hamburger for many years. She is 3-year-old Karen Sue Godsey, who lived on L Street in Sparks. This photo was taken in the original coffee shop in 1957. The Awful Awful got its name from a young customer in Dick Graves' Idaho Coffee Shop who thought the hamburger was "awful-awful good."

hamburger. A look back at an old menu shows a steak sandwich at $1.15, ham-bacon-sausage and eggs at $1 and the Awful-Awful was 65 cents, including the french fries.

The Round House, specializing in mahogany-grilled steaks and chops, opened six months after the coffee shop. It was named in recognition of Sparks' railroad history.

By the early 1960s, the Nugget's reputation for good food had grown rapidly. Ascuaga continued to introduce new restaurants. The Golden Rooster Room and the Pancake Parlor soon satisfied wider tastes and heavier demand.

When the Nugget expanded to the south side of B Street, Trader Dick's, named after Dick Graves, opened on the northeast corner of B and 12th streets. The Polynesian restaurant moved to the main Nugget building in 1973 and still maintains a large, loyal following.

Ascuaga opened the 600-seat Circus

Room in 1962 and John's Oyster Bar in 1964. The Circus Room, the largest showroom in the area at the time, offered headliner entertainment, cocktails and dinner.

By 1978 when the General Store opened, the Nugget could serve 2,124 diners in its restaurants and another 1,100 people in the banquet facility.

When the Nugget's 29-story hotel tower opened in 1984, the new Rotisserie Buffet had already been winning fans for three months. Again, Ascuaga realized that additional first-class food facilities were necessary to keep hotel guests happy. And the addition of first-class restaurants didn't end with the Rotisserie

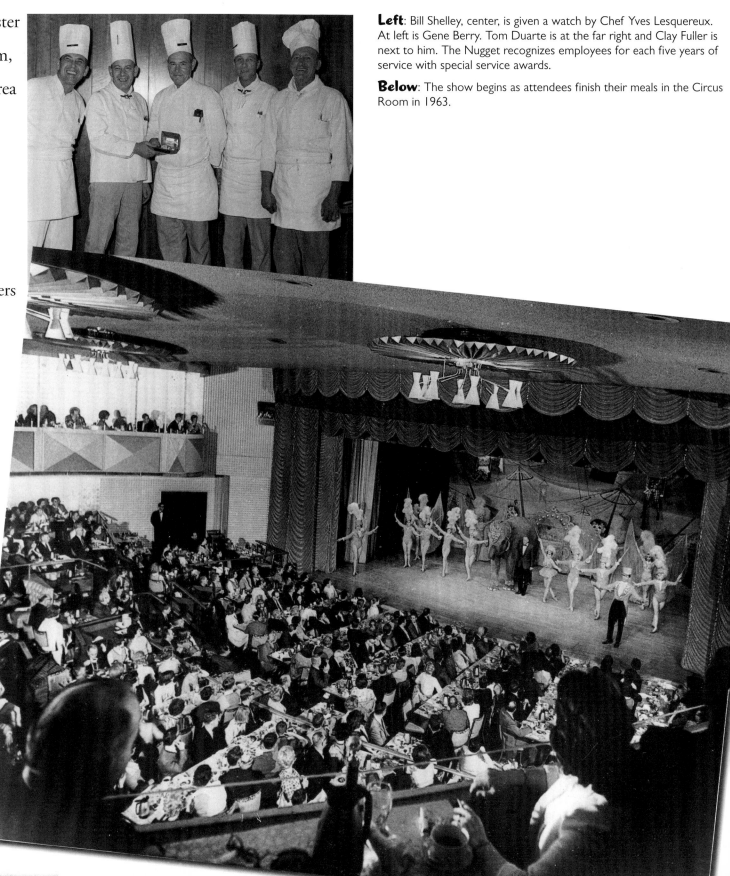

Left: Bill Shelley, center, is given a watch by Chef Yves Lesquereux. At left is Gene Berry. Tom Duarte is at the far right and Clay Fuller is next to him. The Nugget recognizes employees for each five years of service with special service awards.

Below: The show begins as attendees finish their meals in the Circus Room in 1963.

Buffet. Restaurante Orozko opened in 1998 and the General Store, updated and redecorated, became Rosie's Cafe in 2002.

Over the years innumerable chefs, servers and maitre 'ds have contributed to the Nugget's reputation for good food and friendly, efficient service. One, the late Yves Lesquereux, deserves a special mention. The Swiss chef joined the Nugget in 1966 and, as executive chef for more than 30 years, he lent his award-winning culinary magic and management skills to the rapidly expanding dining operations.

As the Nugget celebrates 50 years, eight restaurants continue to prove the adage, "the way to a person's heart is through the stomach": The Farm House (coffee shop), Trader Dick's, The Steakhouse Grill, John's Oyster Bar, The Rotisserie Buffet, Rosie's Cafe, Gabe's Pub & Deli and Restaurante Orozko. Today, at any one time the restaurants can seat 2,500 people and the Rose Ballroom in the convention center can serve 2,000.

Above: Steve Chacon carves a side of roast beef in the Rotisserie Buffet Restaurant at the Nugget in 1985. *Photo by Jean Dixon*

Right: Just three years after the initial coffee shop opened, a 1958 poster inside the Nugget advertises six restaurants.

Left: John Ascuaga and Col. Harland Sanders, two of America's foremost food experts, discuss the fine points of fried chicken in the kitchen of the Golden Rooster Room in 1958. Col. Sanders came to Sparks to demonstrate his unique cooking process to the Nugget.

Below: Yves Lesquereux, right, a familiar figure at John Ascuaga's Nugget, retired in May 1997 after 31 years. Cor Van der Stokker, long time maitre d' in the Circus Room also worked as executive vice president of food and beverage for the Nugget. Both culinary legends worked behind the scenes to make guests dining experiences memorable. Their legacy is continued in the Nugget's eight award-winning restaurants.
Reno Gazette-Journal library.

Below: In 2000, four banquet captains known as the Sparkies had spent 20 years working and laughing together. They are, from left, Marsha Baker, Patti Dettori, Carol Lux and Barbara Murray. *Photo by David B. Parker*

Above: Cook Nelson Martinez cores an onion in preparation for New Year's Eve 2001. About 1,800 onions were used as the "bowl" for the New Year's Eve French Onion soup. *Photo by Liz Margerum*

Left: The Coffee Shop in 1967 featured favorite dishes like the Awful Awful burger and the Nugget's famous fried chicken.

Far Below: Spaciousness and comfort are felt immediately in the newly remodeled 24-hour Coffee Shop in the early 1970s.

Heresto Pands Pen Dasoci Alhou Rinhar M Les Smirt Hand Funl Etfri Ends Hipre Ign Bejus Tand Kindan Devils Peaks of No Ne.

Translation
*Here stop and spend a social hour in harmless mirth and fun;
Let friendship reign, be just and kind, and evil speak of none.*

FARM HOUSE

Above: Since opening in 1958 The Farm House Coffee Shop has featured the above puzzle. The greeting can be seen in the background of the photos on this page and is a favorite of many locals.

The Farm House COFFEE SHOP

RENO AREA'S FINEST

The original coffee shop, called the Farm House, moved south across B Street to the expanded casino site in 1958. It has served guests around the clock throughout the years.

SPECIALTIES

SOUP OF THE DAY	Cup .20	Bowl .35

GROUND ROUND STEAK 1.50
One-Half Pound of Freshly Ground Round Served with Potato and Salad

NUGGET SPECIAL 1.50
OUR SPECIAL STEAK SANDWICH
Delicious Choice Cube Steak coverd with Mushroom Sauce, French Fries and a Green Salad

CHICKEN FRIED STEAK 1.55
America's most popular Steak — Served with Salad, Potato & Hot Roll

FROM THE BROILER

. . . PREPARED FROM CHOICE GRADE AA BEEF . . .

CHUCK WAGON STEAK 1.95
(SMOKE FLAVORED CHOPPED SIRLOIN)
A full half-pound of Choice Chopped Sirloin secretly seasoned, wrapped with Bacon, and broiled. Salad Bowl, Potato and Garlic Bread

JACKPOT STEAK 4.00
U.S. Choice Tenderloin Steak — Salad Bowl and Potato

TOP SIRLOIN STEAK 4.50
U.S. Choice Boneless Steak — Salad Bowl and Potato

NEW YORK STEAK 5.00
U.S. Choice Boneless Steak — Salad Bowl and Potato

SANDWICHES

THE HAMBURGER STORY

We have $3,000.00 in equipment just to grind and patty our Hamburgers . . . using Choice Chuck (shoulder) of Beef and NOT scraps and old odds and ends.

FEATURING OUR FAMOUS . . .

AWFUL-AWFUL .95

A Two Patty Hamburger Feast in a basket with French Fries

¼ POUND HAMBURGER	.65
¼ POUND CHEESEBURGER	.75
FRIED HAM SANDWICH	.85

COLD BEEF SANDWICH	.85
CHEESE SANDWICH	.55
EGG SANDWICH	.55
HAM OR BACON AND EGG	.95
BACON AND TOMATO	.75
"ROAST OF THE DAY" SANDWICH	1.25

A hot Sandwich made from the Roast we are featuring today.

NUGGET'S AWARD WINNING RESTAURANTS

ROUND HOUSE
Specializing in Steaks, Chops and Seafood

PANCAKE PARLOR
World famous recipes of Pancakes and Waffles, plus Steaks and Chicken

GOLDEN ROOSTER ROOM
Featuring Golden Rooster Fried Chicken, Nuggets of Tenderloin Steak and Prime Rib

JOHN'S OYSTER BAR
Ocean Fresh Oysters and other Seafoods flown in fresh daily

TRADER DICK'S
Chinese dinners and fantabulous Steaks (Located across the street from the Nugget)

CIRCUS ROOM THEATER RESTAURANT
Sumptuous dining and fabulous entertainment night

SALADS

Choice of French, Roquefort or Thousand Island Dressing

NUGGET SEASHORE SALAD

Freshly cut Mixed Greens topped with generous se of three delectable seafoods . . . Crab, Shrimp and Lo Served with your choice of Dressings.

$2.25

CHEF'S SPECIAL SALAD BOWL

Garden fresh Mixed Greens topped with Julienne of Ham, Breast of Turkey, Swiss Cheese, Hard-boiled Egg and Tomatoes. Served with your choice of Dressings.

$1.85

NUGGET TROPICAL FRUIT BOWL

One quarter of a Fresh Pineapple topped with Cott Cheese surounded by Bananas, Peaches, Pears Grapes and other Fresh Fruits and four dainty Peanut Butter Sandwiches.

$2.25

Above: Coffee Shop menu. (1962)

A 15-pound, 18-karat solid gold rooster marked the entrance of the Golden Rooster Room restaurant that opened in the early 1960s and became famous for its fried chicken. Open for lunch and dinner, the restaurant featured a complete menu and a hot and cold buffet. The area was remodeled and reopened as The Rotisserie Buffet in 1984. The rooster, in a glass case, now struts its stuff in the hotel. Newman's Silver Shop of Reno and Shreve's of San Francisco were commissioned to create the rooster from a model created by sculptor-artist Frank Polk.

Left: A favorite luncheon spot for businessmen was the Buffet in the Golden Rooster Room. The restaurant was a popular after school work place for University of Nevada, Reno students. (1973)

Above: The Round House Restaurant featured steaks, chops and seafood and was one of the most popular at the Nugget.

Right: The Steakhouse Grill's vintage European bistro décor invites diners to linger over dinner. (2004) *Photo by Richard Stokes*

Specializing in mahogany-grilled steaks, chops and seafood, the Round House opened in 1956. In 1991 the room was remodeled and named The Steakhouse Grill. Over three million steaks have been served since 1956.

The Pancake Parlor, opened in 1960, featured more than 60 kinds of pancakes from around the world and offered a complete breakfast, lunch and dinner menu. This room gave way to an expanded Oyster Bar in 1979.

PANCAKE PARLOR

Over 25 varieties of world-famous poncakes, waffles, regular breakfasts, chicken and steaks. Open: 7 am to 10 pm – 7 days a week

Below: Offering a menu that included 60 different pancakes and a complete variety of breakfast and coffee shop items made the Pancake Parlor a "first choice" for many Nugget customers.

Left: John Ascuaga is all smiles at the grand opening of Trader Dick's. Delicious Polynesian food, live music, dancing and exotic Island drinks have made Trader Dick's an area favorite date spot.

Top Right: Frank Polk, who designed the famous Golden Rooster, carves the golden dragon before the opening of the unique tiki-themed Trader Dick's.

Bottom Right: The tropical island décor, unique to Reno-Sparks, quickly made Trader Dick's a popular dining spot. Here, customers enjoy their dining experience at the grand opening.

Trader Dick's opened in 1958, moved into the main building in 1973 and into its present location in 1988. Island artifacts, a vivid blue and green color scheme and an enormous aquarium announce the entrance to this Polynesian dinner room. Exotic entrees and cocktails fill the menu.

Above: Trader Dick's staff members Chef Jimmy Chinn, left, Maitre 'd John S.W. Chen and Chef Tom Wong. (1967)

Right: Trader Dick's features jungle-like plants and dark, moody lighting. In 2002, the menu was updated to include Pan-Asian specialties in addition to the Polynesian favorites. *Photo by David B. Parker*

Below: Pastry chef Didier Laborde shows off one of his creations in October 2002. *Photo by Richard Stokes*

Below Right: The aquarium at John Ascuaga's Nugget holds 30,000 gallons of water and is home to over 100 fish. Built right underneath I-80 the "coral" in the fish tank are actually a part of the freeway support system.

In 1962, Ascuaga added entertainment with a 600-seat showroom, The Circus Room. It featured a full dinner menu and headliner show. The room later was re-named the Celebrity Showroom. Bertha, the elephant, was the opening act until her death in 1999.

Opening in June! The Circus Room, A 600 SEAT THEATER RESTAURANT

NUGGET Casino-Motor Lodge SPARKS

Right: Cor Van der Stokker, maitre d' in the Circus Room at John Ascuaga's Nugget, and his staff of five captains in 1975 had a combined total of 65 years of continuous employment at the Nugget. Checking menus and seating charts before a dinner show are, from left, Jim Mihalek, Dave Ahlberg, Mike Suarez, Cor Van der Stokker, Brian O'Toole and Flyn Somday.

Below: Stagehands, stars, captains, waiters, waitresses, bus boys, bartenders, cooks and dishwashers — this is the crew it took to put together a dinner show in the Circus Room in the 1960s.

Bottom: Tony Lubbers, left, and Gene Berry watch over the special steam cookers offering exhibition cooking at the Oyster Bar Counter in 1973. These cookers are famous for making John's Oyster Bar's signature dish, the pan roast — a cream-based seafood stew.

John's Oyster Bar opened in 1964 and specializes in fresh shellfish, flown in daily and served in a nautical setting. Seafood gets the spotlight in stews, pan roasts, salads and seafood cocktails. Open daily for lunch and dinner, seating was expanded from 57 to 125 when it moved to the old Pancake Parlor location in 1979.

JOHN'S OYSTER BAR
"WELCOME ABOARD"

Ice Cold Clam Juice	.30	Chilled Tomato Juice	.30
Piping Hot Clam Broth	.50		

FRESHLY SHUCKED OYSTERS ON THE HALF SHELL

Flown directly from Louisiana and served to you on a bed of crushed ice.

One-half dozen New Orleans Grand Bayou $1.85

Jumbo Shrimp Cocktail	$1.35	Baby Shrimp Cocktail	$1.35
Tender Sweet Lobster Cocktail	1.60	Crab Meat Cocktail	1.35
Freshly Shucked Oyster Cocktail	1.90	Cracked Alaska King Crab on a bed or crushed ice	2.00

Your choice of John's Cocktail Sauce or Hot Mustard Sauce

JOHN'S OYSTER STEW
$1.85

A steaming, fragrant bowl full made with fresh shucked oysters, cooked in butter, cream and fine spices and seasonings.

MANHATTAN CLAM CHOWDER

Bowl	.60	Cup	.35

Served with our own French bread and butter or crisp Trenton crackers.

NEW YORK'S FAMOUS PAN ROASTS

This is the aristocrat of all stews and is cooked to your order with the very finest of spices, Chablis wine, clam broth, cream, butter, special cocktail sauce, drop of lemon and your choice of fresh seafood.

Oyster Pan Roast	2.35
Clam Pan Roast	2.35
Lobster Pan Roast	2.60
Shrimp Pan Roast	2.35
Combination Pan Roast	2.60

JOHN'S FAVORITE GUMBO FILE A LA CREOLE

Served with French Bread and Butter.

A succulent stew made from fresh seafood, imported spices and rice and served steaming hot at your table. A favorite on the Louisiana plantation for over two hundred years.

$1.55

Rich Clam Stew	1.85	Tender Lobster Stew	2.10
Alaska Shrimp Stew	1.85	Combination Seafood Stew	2.10

Crisp Seafood Salads

Large Crab Louie	2.25	Alaska Shrimp Louie	2.25
King Size Lobster Louie	2.75	Combination Seafood Louie	2.75

You can taste the tang of the salty air — magnificently garnished and served on a large Salad Platter.

STEM TO STERN

Coffee	.15	Our Delicious Apple Pie	.35
Tea	.15	with Cheese	.45
Milk	.15	House Specialty — Pecan Pie	.35

TO COMPLEMENT YOUR MEAL, MAY WE SUGGEST MICHELOB BEER ON DRAUGHT?

Right: Waitresses in John's Oyster Bar all sported hard hats for the construction of the Nugget's first tower.

Above: In 1997, Claudia Green (left) and Ruth Jensen, were two of the many long-time waitresses in the Oyster Bar — Green 29 years and Jensen 31. The crew of the Oyster Bar are like family and treat the customers the same. The wait staff is so efficient that many regulars get their favorite dish and drink delivered before they even order.

Left: John's Oyster Bar menu. (1967)

Left: Chickens roasting at the Rotisserie Buffet entrance draw in diners with a delicious aroma. The tablecloth dining experience is more upscale than other buffets in the region. Every night of the week features something different, from prime rib to fresh fish to Chinese to rib night to King Crab, the Rotisserie Buffet's food quality and variety are second to none. (2004)

Right: Diners load up their plates at the Rotisserie Buffet in 1997. The Rotisserie Buffet opened in 1984, just before the first hotel tower. Reno/Sparks residents voted it the area's best buffet for more than 10 years straight. *Photo by Mark Studyvin*

Opened in 1984 just ahead of the Nugget's first hotel tower, the buffet, decorated in wood, tile, glass and lots of copper and brass, features roast duck, roast beef, spit-roasted chicken and salads, vegetables, side dishes and desserts laid out for as far as the eye can see.

When the Race & Sports Book was expanded, this pub and deli was added to the lower-level Pavilion. The deli is named after John Ascuaga's eldest grandchild, Gabriel.

Above: The Farm House. (2004)

Right: Named after John's grandson and Camille's son, Gabriel, Gabe's Deli opened in April 1994 on the lower level adjacent to the Race and Sportsbook. Gabe's Deli was added to service the Nugget's growing convention business, which often demands quick take-out orders. The deli offers snacks, breakfast, lunch and dinner items.

"The Shepherd," an impressive sculpture representing the sheepherders' way of life and the spirit of the Basque people, stands at the entrance of the dinner room. Opened in 1998, the lovely décor and the menu continue the Basque theme with some of the recipes coming directly from the Ascuaga family.

Center: Restaurante Orozko gives the feeling of outdoor dining with its sky ceiling, trees and café setting. Guests can partake in a traditional Basque Picon Punch at the Orozko lounge, which features live instrumental music. *Photo by Joe Gosen*

Top Right: In 2003, the Pyrenees Room was opened in the back of Restaurante Orozko. This popular party and meeting room has the feel of the restaurant.

Bottom Right: An advertisement for the opening of Restaurante Orozko in 1998.

Left: A Sheepherder's Statue.

Above: Entrance to Rosie's Cafe, the Nugget's 24-hour coffee shop. (2004) *Photo by Richard Stokes*

Right: Two ice sculptures of the Nugget's celebrated elephants were created for the resort's 49th anniversary celebration. (2004)

This restaurant is open around the clock and offers a diverse selection of breakfast, lunch and dinner choices. Opened in 1978 as The General Store it was completely remodeled and named Rosie's Cafe in 2002.

Below: The Nugget's famous Strawberry Festival began in 1964 and features strawberry delights including strawberry shortcake. Eight-year-old Laurel Cooney, also known as the strawberry girl, is used in advertising for the month-long summer celebration. (2000)

Bottom: The view as customers enter Rosie's Cafe. (2004) *Photo by Richard Stokes*

When the General Store became Rosie's Cafe, most changes were cosmetic. Spaces were reworked to make service more efficient and the décor became more colorful and modern. But the family-friendly menu, with some updates, remained in place. Yes, the Awful Awful still is a best-seller. The restaurant is named after Michonne Ascuaga's daughter.

Entertainment

John Ascuaga's Nugget has always been a premiere location in Northern Nevada for entertainment. In 1962, the Nugget opened a 600-seat theater, complete with balcony seating, and called it The Circus Room, both to imply an atmosphere of fun and to accommodate its regular performer, Bertha, the Nugget's trademark elephant. The show opening night was International Follies.

Thus began more than four decades of major headliner entertainment wherein the Circus Room, renamed the Celebrity Showroom in 1977 (and for a brief period the Celebrity Cabaret in 1986) hosted the biggest and brightest of the entertainment world, its roster over the years a virtual who's who of who was and is hot.

Liberace provided extravagant productions, including the extraordinary

Above: "King of the Road" Roger Miller brought his musical and storytelling talents to the Circus Room.

Right: Roy Clark pickin' and grinnin' at the Nugget. (2000)

HAPPY 63rd
RED!
From our Friends at the Nugge

This Photo: John Ascuaga helped let everyone know that friend and performer Red Skelton was turning 63 with a large billboard. (1976)

Dancing Waters, a lighted fountain display on stage that moved to his music. Red Skelton brought his warmth, humor, and cast of characters from Clem Kadidlehopper to the Mean Widdle Kid. Juliet Prowse performed elegant extended dances to music such as "Bolero." Dick Martin heckled Dan Rowan's attempt to recite from Shakespeare. And Shirley MacLaine performed the choreography of Michael Kidd and Jerome Robbins.

Kate Smith sang "God Bless America," making the Nugget the only casino where she ever performed. The Mills Brothers provided classic swing vocals. Al Hirt brought New Orleans jazz to Sparks. Raquel Welch brought movie-star glamour. Lorne Greene, Dan Blocker, and Michael Landon came in from the Ponderosa. Movie and television and recording

Right: Two of America's clowns — Emmett Kelly and Red Skelton — were popular attractions in the Circus Room at the Nugget.

PANCAKE PARLOR
SOUVENIR MENU

OFFICIAL PUBLICATION OF
JOHN ASCUAGA'S NUGGET

Menu

NUGGET GAZETTE

JANUARY 1972   JOHN ASCUAGA'S NUGGET   SPARKS, NEVADA

★★ Circus Room '72 Stars ★★

Ed Ames   Carol Channing   Liberace   Juliet Prowse

Marty Robbins   Jimmy Dean

Sandler & Young   Kreskin   Skiles & Henderson   Buck Owens

stars were, in fact, everywhere — Ginger Rogers, Andy Williams, Debbie Reynolds, Pearl Bailey, Danny Thomas, Jimmy Durante, Burl Ives, Nancy Sinatra, Rick Nelson, Ray Conniff, Carol Channing, Fred Waring and His Pennsylvanians, Frankie Laine, Dinah Shore, Johnny Mathis, the Johnny Mann Singers, Ed Ames, Andy Griffith, Frankie Avalon — the list and variety are both endless.

It was at the Nugget where country music began to make inroads into casino entertainment. For a long time, it was considered too backwoods for sophisticated environments, but the Nugget began booking talents like Roy Clark and Mel Tillis and the Oak Ridge Boys. The old pea picker himself, Tennessee Ernie Ford, was a favorite, as were Glen Campbell, Crystal Gayle, Louise Mandrell and Kris Kristofferson. Country music became not only a permanent presence at the Nugget, but around the state.

Patrons made reservations, lined up to be seated by longtime maitre d' Cor Van der Stokker, and attended either a dinner show, which began at 8 p.m., or a cocktail show, which began at 11 p.m. The early show was family-oriented; the late show more adult, although John Ascuaga would not allow much blue material at any time. The room staff somehow managed between the hours of 6 p.m. and 8 p.m. nightly to provide 900 patrons with cocktails, salad, dinner, dessert, coffee, and after-dinner drinks before clearing the floor so as not to disturb the entertainer. It was a feat that required the planning and execution of a major military operation.

An evening in the theater guaranteed elegance. There was a house orchestra, first led by Leighton Noble and then by Don Conn. They provided both dinner music and support for whatever musical guest was appearing. For the first few years, there was even a dance line, a holdover of the club tradition begun in places like New York's Copacabana and the Latin Quarter. The Nugget hosted the Dorothy Dorben Dancers, who performed an opening number, usually just following Bertha, and often joined in the shows themselves if the headliner required it.

Shows followed a fairly regular format. If the headliner was a singer, the opening act almost invariably was a comedian and vice versa. Many stars cut their teeth in the room. Steve Martin was an opening act for Roger Miller, for instance. There were brief flings with revues, like "Hi-Heel Sneakers," but even they tended to feature stars.

The Celebrity Showroom since 2000 has opened for weekend and special shows and contemporary major draws perform in the Rose Ballroom. Entertainment has hardly been restricted to the main showroom at the Nugget, however. In 1974 the Casino Cabaret was opened and over the years it provided a wide variety of entertainment, from stars like Anna Maria Alberghetti and JoAnn Castle, to revues like "Naughty, But Nice" and "Jubilation," to debuts of future stars like Natalie Cole and Pam Tillis. In 1985, the enclosed space was opened to the casino. Smaller ensembles and single entertainers have performed around the club, in Trader Dick's Lounge for instance, and in the bar area of Restaurante Orozko.

Entertainment also has gone outdoors. For 16 years the Nugget

Right: Louise Mandrell performs in the Celebrity Showroom. (1985) *Photo by Marilyn Newton*

has hosted the Best in the West Nugget Rib Cook-Off and provided free entertainment on multiple stages with major stars every evening.

Nugget entertainment may have changed with the times, but it's always been an essential part of the total gaming-resort experience and its rich history promises to continue into the future.

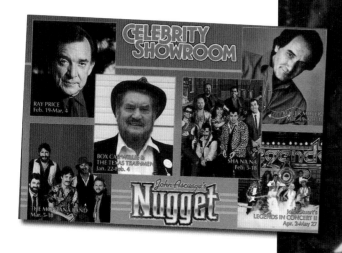

Above: The Celebrity Showroom featured many stars.

Right: Bertha and Liberace make their entrance in the Circus Room (1973).

Left: Debbie Reynolds showcased her multiple talents in the Circus Room in 1976.

Above: Glen Campbell has been a regular headliner in the Celebrity Showroom for several decades.

Above: The Oak Ridge Boys played the Celebrity Showroom in 1980. Their career took off at the Nugget.

Left: Leggy Juliet Prowse twirls up a storm on the Circus Room stage.

Center: Nugget postcard featuring Danny Thomas' performance.

Below: Dancers practice during a rehearsal for "Sheep Dip 40" on stage in the Celebrity Showroom in January 2004. *Photo by Liz Margerum*

Danny Thomas

Lola Falana

CELEBRITY ROOM THEATER RESTAURANT
NUGGET

Left: Pam Tillis, Mel Tillis' daughter, has gravitated from the Casino Cabaret to the Celebrity Showroom.

Above: Nugget postcards featuring the performance of Mel Tillis, Bobby Goldsboro, Golddiggers, Conway Twitty and the Lennon Sisters.

Left: Raquel Welch displayed her song and dance talents on the Circus Room stage.

Center: Barbara Eden performs at the Nugget.

Below: Kate Smith sang "God Bless America." The Nugget was the only casino where she ever performed.

Appearing July 15-22

Barbara Eden

John Ascuaga's Nugget

Above: Shirley MacLaine sang, danced, soliloquized and performed parts from her movies at the Nugget.

Middle: Natalie Cole's first appearance at the Nugget was in the Casino Cabaret.

Right: Rowan and Martin's stage show at the Nugget was every bit as funny as their hit television series, "Laugh-In."

Above: The Cabaret opened in 1974, when it was enclosed with glass that was curtained during performances and a maitre d' seated guests.

Right: "Jubilation," a musical revue, came to the Casino Cabaret in 1978.

Left: Red Skelton celebrated his 82nd birthday at the Nugget in July 1995. *Photo by Marilyn Newton*

Above: Miss Nevada pageant contestants surround the 1999 winner, Gina Giacinto of Las Vegas, whose back is to the camera, after she was announced on stage in the Celebrity Showroom. *Photo by Scott Sady*

Left: Carol Channing, longtime headliner in the Circus Room..

Left: Wayne Newton in concert June 5, 2004, in the Rose Ballroom. *Photo by Marilyn Newton.*

Below: Ray Charles was a popular performer in the Rose Ballroom at John Ascuaga's Nugget. (1994)

Left: Johnny Cash performed in the Rose Ballroom in 1995.

Above: An audience of nearly 2,000 enjoy the Johnny Cash concert from the back of the Rose Ballroom in 1995.

Above: The Nugget has hosted thousands of entertainers in the Circus Room, which later was renamed the Celebrity Showroom. Guests can see the entertainment of the years with this postcard display that is located just outside the Celebrity Showroom.

Nugget: A birds-eye view of entertainers and more

JOHN AT THE WHEEL: John Ascuaga gets work started on the first Nugget tower.

Provided by Ruthie Jensen

Many fond memories at landmark

NUGGET TOWER GRAND OPENING DEC. 26 1984

From page 1

of celebrities including Skelton — who always ordered oyster stew — Lorne Greene, Pat Boone, Tennessee Ernie Ford and others.

"I just love being around people," Jensen said. "I like serving them and seeing them happy and listening to their stories."

Above all, both Jensen and Neuschwander say they cherish the camaraderie shared with John Ascuaga and the lighthearted kidding he often gives them.

"When he comes in, he always says: 'Ruthie get to work, Alma get to work,'" Neuschwander said. "Oh, he'll say: 'I want to sit anywhere but in Ruthie's station'" and then, of course, he goes and sits in Ruthie's station."

McKinney said she is most grateful for the career opportunities extended her by the Nugget. In 1977, the then 47-year-old was promoted to the position of showroom captain. The move wasn't popular with the then maitre d' but enthusiastically endorsed by Ascuaga.

"I wasn't a woman libber but I thought I had the experience," said McKinney who became the first woman in northern Nevada to be named to the position. "At that time, a woman at the door wasn't the thing but Ms. Ascuaga

thought it was a good idea so I was promoted."

That opportunity gave her a birds-eye view of the showroom's entertainers. Her favorites included Red Skelton and Liberace. McKinney said she adored Liberace's costumes and jewelry — and his sense of humor.

"He'd say (during a show) to the people sitting down front: 'You want to see my jewelry?'" recalled McKinney who was promoted to maitre d' in 1987. "Sure you can see it see it, you paid for it."

Both Jensen and

IN THE TRUNK: Aggie McKinney is hoisted aloft by Bertha at the Convention Center in Reno.

Provided by Aggie McKinney

Neuschwander say one of the highlights of their tenure at Nugget includes the construction of the property's first tower.

"We (employees) all got to go outside — almost shut us down," said Neuschwander who kept her hard hat and other commemorative souvenirs associated with the event.

Likewise, both say one of the casino's saddest days occurred when Bertha died in November 1999.

"That was awful," Jensen said. "We all cried."

And, they've had a chance to see the Ascuaga children mature

HOWDY: Aggie McKinney and Jimmy Dean (before he made sausage.)

Provided by Aggie McKinney

of adulthood.

"We've seen Michonne, and Stephen and John Jr. grow up," said Neuschwander, who fondly recalls seeing the trio dressed up when attending holiday events. Most of all McKinney, Jensen

YOU'RE INVITED

In honor of its 48th anniversary, the Nugget is celebrating with free cake and coffee for its guests.

When: 3 p.m., March 17

Where: John Ascuaga's Nugget Celebrity Showroom

Details: (775) 356-3300

Provided by Aggie McKinney

FUN TIMES: Aggie McKinney, at left, is all smiles with Liberace. Above, she is decked out as Nurse Hoolihan as the Nugget marked the end of television's M*A*S*H series.

and take on the responsibilities

and Neuschwander say working at the Nugget is a source of pride for them.

"People love coming to the

Nugget," McKinney said. "When I say I work at the Nugget I'm proud because I think John runs a good place."

THE NUGGET AT 48

THE OLD GANG: Waitresses in John's Oyster Bar all sport hard hats for the construction of the Nugget's first tower.

Provided by Ruthie Jensen

Longtime employees love their work

By Alison Bath
RENO GAZETTE-JOURNAL
abath@rgj.com

For Aggie McKinney, 39 years of working at John Ascuaga's Nugget means lots of memories. Sitting in the casino's darkened Celebrity Showroom — where she began her career as a cocktail waitress in 1964 — McKinney sifts through those reminiscences that are immortalized in cards, photographs and other memorabilia.

There are snapshots of McKinney with comedic impersonator Red Skelton and flamboyant pianist Liberace. There's one of her receiving a giant bear hug from country western entertainer Jimmy Dean and another catches McKinney perched on Bertha's — the Nugget's elephant mascot — trunk.

And, a perusal through McKinney's collection reveals dozens and dozens of glossy studio shots of the entertainers who frequently appeared in the showroom. There's Dottie West, Nell Carter, Brenda Lee and Roy Clark, and groups such as The Letterman, The McGuire Sisters and The Oak Ridge Boys — each picture signed and inscribed with a personal message to McKinney.

"We go back a long ways," said McKinney as she looked at photographs of forgotten stars Patty Page and TJ Sheppard.

Like McKinney, many of the Nugget's oldest-serving employees have seen the Sparks landmark grow over the years. They've shared in its triumphs – the addition of towers and restaurants – and they've grieved at its misfortunes – the death of Bertha and a 1993 bomb threat that forced the evacuation of 6,000 guests.

SERVING UP MEMORIES: Longtime Nugget employees are John's Oyster Bar waitresses Ruthie Jensen, right, and Alma Neuschwander. Jensen has worked at the Nugget since 1966 and Neuschwander has worked there since 1973.

Tim Dunn/Reno Gazette

GOOD EVENING: Aggie McKinney is an icon at the Nugget. She was the first female maitre d' in northern Nevada.

Candice Towell/Reno Gazette-Journal

And as the Nugget prepares to celebrate 48 years in northern Nevada this Monday, they're thrilled to have been a part of it all.

"I just think I'm very, very fortunate," McKinney said. "I've worked for a nice family

... I can't say enough nice things about the Nugget."

McKinney along with fellow employees Ruthie Jensen and Alma Neuschwander have spent the better part of their careers working for the man they affectionately call "Mr. A."

If you ask them why they've spent so many years at one job, they'll simply tell you there's no place they'd rather be.

"What else would I do?" asks Jensen, a waitress at John's Oyster Bar who has worked at the Nugget since 1966. "It's not

like work — it's a pleasure," Jensen said it's not only a chance to see celebrities and part of the Nugget's history, the opportunity to build relationships with her customers and fellow employees and customers has made her job fun.

She and Neuschwander, fellow Oyster Bar waitresses, joined the Nugget staff, fondly talk about regular customers who have shared their lives with the pair. Jensen and Neuschwander, they've helped celebrate marriages and the birth of children and been on hand to lend a sympathetic ear if a customer's loved one or other misfortunes befell. And, those customers don't have to worry.

"I can't repeat that," said. "You don't repeat — that's a confidence." The duo has also been

See **NUGGET** or

For Aggie McKinney, working at John Ascuaga's Nugget has been a memorable experience. She began her career as a cocktail waitress in 1964. In 1977, she was promoted to showroom captain — a move that was endorsed enthusiastically by Ascuaga as she became the first woman in Northern Nevada to be named to that position.

McKinney broke the gender barrier again in 1987 when she was promoted to maitre d' of the Celebrity Showroom — again, the first woman in Northern Nevada to hold that position, and it's a job she still holds today.

Above: Herb Reed and the Platters sing the group's classics at a concert in the Celebrity Showroom in 1999. *Photo by Marilyn Newton*

Near Right: Andy Williams croons in the Circus Room in the 1960s.

Far Right: The Lettermen on stage in the Celebrity Showroom in 1998. *Photo by Marilyn Newton*

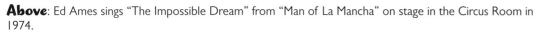

Above: Ed Ames sings "The Impossible Dream" from "Man of La Mancha" on stage in the Circus Room in 1974.

Above Right: Ginger Rogers sang and danced in the Circus Room in the 1960s.

Right: Country singer Crystal Gayle has been a regular in the Celebrity Showroom.

Bertha

Above: Bertha has her own stogie with comedian George Burns.

Right: Angel, the new elephant at the Nugget, in December 1989, is fed a bottle of non-fat baby formula by trainer Don Bloomer. Angel joined Bertha as a performer in early 1990. *Photo by David B. Parker*

Many families can point with pride and nostalgia at marks on door jambs where they've chronicled their children's growth. Many families in Reno-Sparks can point to different gauges — pictures of their children over the years alongside Bertha, the Nugget's longtime resident performing elephant.

Bertha worked her way into the hearts of the community from her arrival in 1962 to her retirement and subsequent death in 1999 at the age of 48. She was the symbol and resident of the Nugget's Circus Room (and later Celebrity Showroom). She became the longest-running casino act in Nevada history, and her appearances in area parades and at every special holiday event made her one of the area's best-known celebrities. There is hardly an elementary school in northern Nevada she did not visit.

This Photo: Bertha and Tamara Geltmaker on stage in the Celebrity Room in 1980.

It was difficult to miss her. An elephant-crossing sign was erected on Nugget Avenue across from her longtime residence, the elephant barn (which hardly looked like a barn, more like a circus residence for the boss), and she was seen going back and forth to her performances, led by a series of trainers and keepers.

There was hardly a show in the Nugget's main showroom spanning nearly four decades in which Bertha did not appear, usually opening the evening, showing off her balancing skills, her musical skills (she played a mean horn, drum, and keyboard), and her gentle manner lifting a long line of female assistants in her mouth. As the years went on and her arthritis began to take a bigger toll, her more challenging tricks went to the wayside, but she remained a favorite no matter what she did.

Top: Bertha and Tina lived in what was referred to as the Bertha Barn, pictured here in 1973.

Bottom: Bertha greets presidential candidate Richard Nixon in 1968.

Bertha shared the stage with more entertainers than practically anyone in show business can claim. She carried an elegantly garbed Liberace on stage ("Wasn't that spectacular?" he asked the audience. "Wasn't that just spectacular? And did you notice the elephant?") At the end of most of her performances, she would take a step toward the audience and lift a banner welcoming whatever headliner was appearing that evening. Most of them would then incorporate a reference to her in their act, having never shared a stage with an elephant anywhere else.

John Ascuaga acquired Bertha, born in India, for $8,000 from a circus museum in Wisconsin. Bertha performed with Tina, a younger elephant, another Tina when the first one grew too large to continue the act, and finally Angel, her little stage mate at the end. She appeared on many national television shows such as Ed Sullivan, Steve Allen and Dinah Shore. Her likeness was made into whiskey decanters and her paintings were sold in the Nugget Gift Shop. For years, she had a fan club and its members received birthday cards with her footprint signature.

There are no elephants at the Nugget anymore. The barn has been dismantled. Bertha's presence, however, is still remembered. She was an essential part of the atmosphere and the community for too long to be forgotten.

Above: Bertha and Last Chance Joe at Christmas time in 1969.

This Photo: Bertha and Tina with trainer C.J. Madison coax some treats from young visitors in 1969. Bertha was a favorite among kids of all ages.

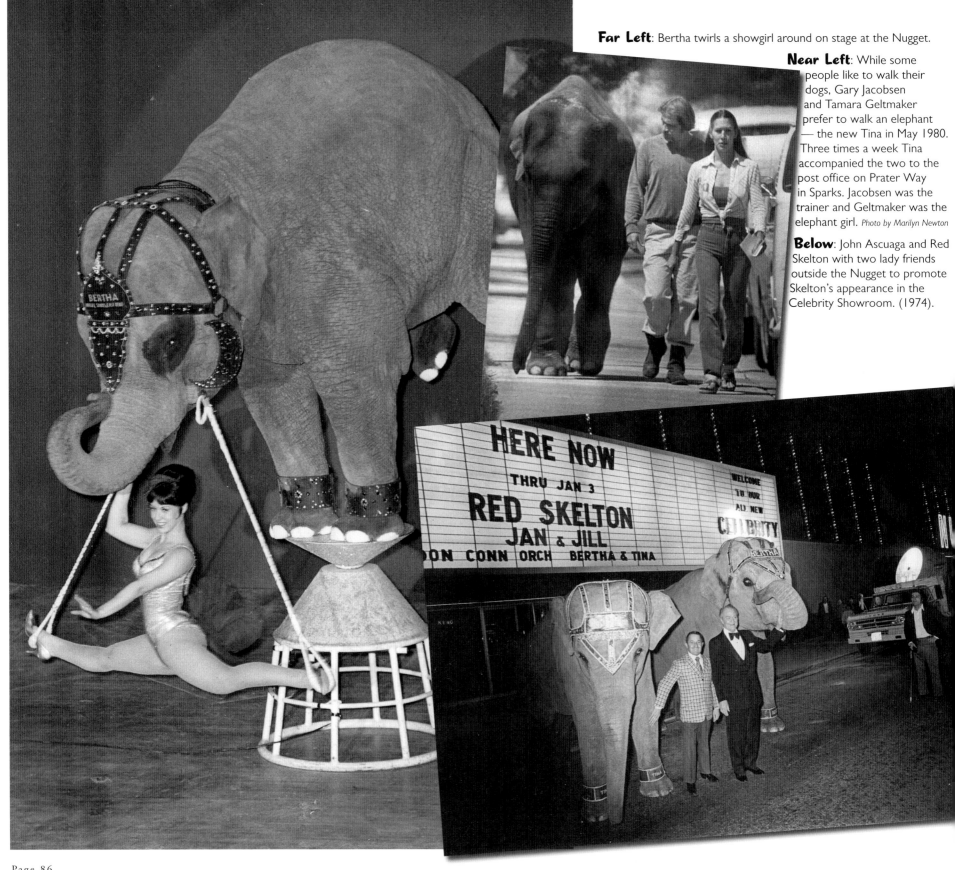

Far Left: Bertha twirls a showgirl around on stage at the Nugget.

Near Left: While some people like to walk their dogs, Gary Jacobsen and Tamara Geltmaker prefer to walk an elephant — the new Tina in May 1980. Three times a week Tina accompanied the two to the post office on Prater Way in Sparks. Jacobsen was the trainer and Geltmaker was the elephant girl. *Photo by Marilyn Newton*

Below: John Ascuaga and Red Skelton with two lady friends outside the Nugget to promote Skelton's appearance in the Celebrity Showroom. (1974).

HERE NOW
THRU JAN 3
RED SKELTON
JAN & JILL
DON CONN ORCH BERTHA & TINA
WELCOME TO OUR ALL NEW CELEBRITY

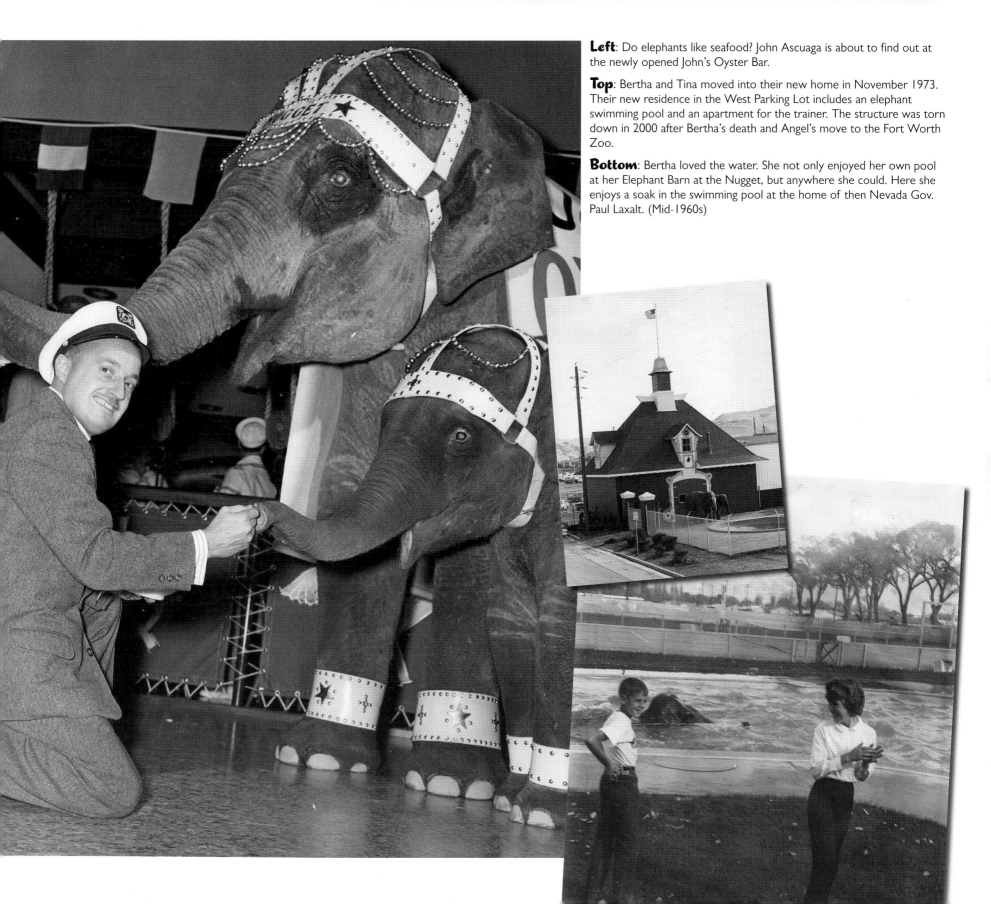

Left: Do elephants like seafood? John Ascuaga is about to find out at the newly opened John's Oyster Bar.

Top: Bertha and Tina moved into their new home in November 1973. Their new residence in the West Parking Lot includes an elephant swimming pool and an apartment for the trainer. The structure was torn down in 2000 after Bertha's death and Angel's move to the Fort Worth Zoo.

Bottom: Bertha loved the water. She not only enjoyed her own pool at her Elephant Barn at the Nugget, but anywhere she could. Here she enjoys a soak in the swimming pool at the home of then Nevada Gov. Paul Laxalt. (Mid-1960s)

Top Left: Bertha was a star outside the showroom, too. She represented the Nugget in hundreds of appearances at local and regional events and festivals. Bertha is pictured here performing at the Modoc County Fair in Alturas, Calif., in August 1990.

Left: Bertha greets new arrival Angel in 1989.

Above: For Bertha's daily walks, an elephant crossing sign was installed near her home.

This Photo: The Harlem Globetrotters faced the most formidable opponent of their career in an exhibition game in Reno when they faced off with Bertha in 1979. After claiming "foul," Bertha proved her talents on the court by sinking a free throw.

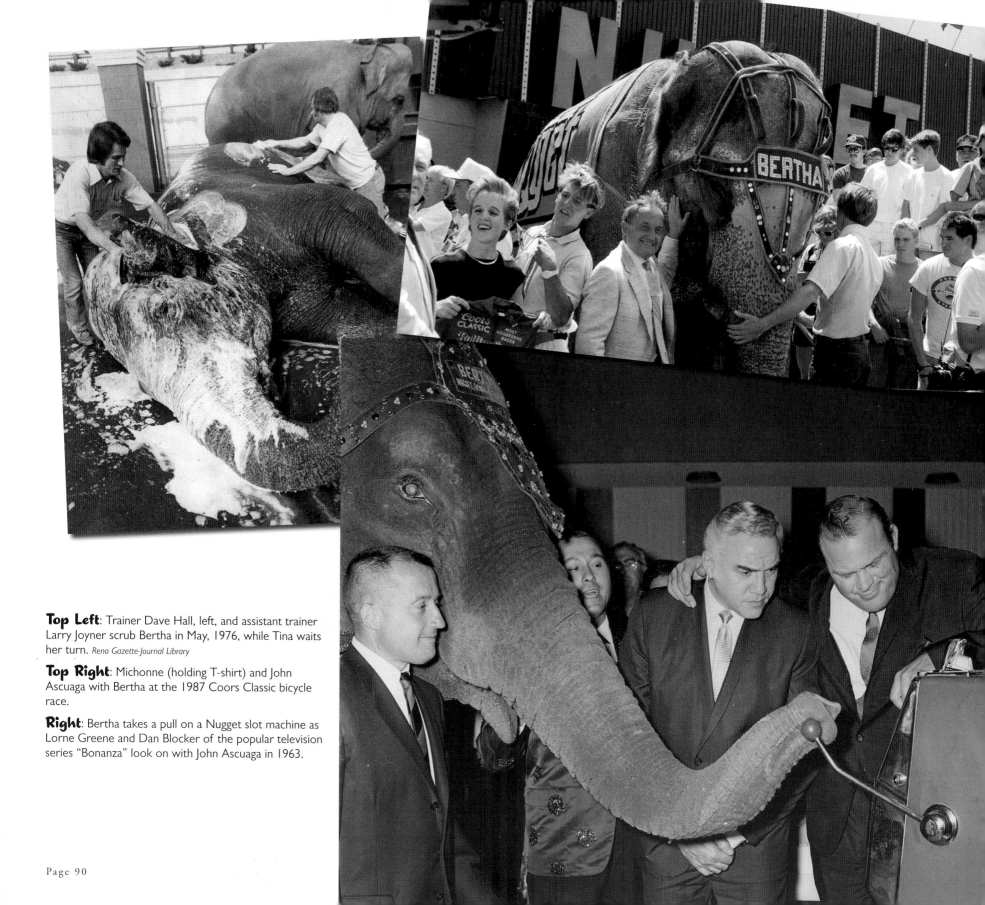

Top Left: Trainer Dave Hall, left, and assistant trainer Larry Joyner scrub Bertha in May, 1976, while Tina waits her turn. *Reno Gazette-Journal Library*

Top Right: Michonne (holding T-shirt) and John Ascuaga with Bertha at the 1987 Coors Classic bicycle race.

Right: Bertha takes a pull on a Nugget slot machine as Lorne Greene and Dan Blocker of the popular television series "Bonanza" look on with John Ascuaga in 1963.

Angel packs trunk for trip to new Texas home

By Faith Bremner
RENO GAZETTE-JOURNAL

Angel the elephant is being prepared this week for a move to Texas.

The last performing elephant at John Ascuaga's Nugget, 11-year-old Angel will start a new life at the Fort Worth Zoo's nationally-recognized Asian elephant breeding program.

It's the best place for her to be after her adopted sister, Bertha, died Nov. 10 at age 48, said Stephen Ascuaga, Nugget senior vice president.

"It's sad but it's in her best interest," Ascuaga said. "She'll do well with the elephants there. She's just entering her breeding years. One of the major reasons we're sending her there is she'll be able to experience having a baby."

The zoo has five Asian elephants: Groucho, a lone bull; Babe, Kimbo, Rasha and her new calf, Bluebonnet. The elephants live in a 3.5-acre enclosure that includes a 3,200-square-foot pool and a house big enough for eight elephants.

Angel will travel to Texas over two or three days in a climate-controlled truck built

Tim Dunn/Reno Gazette-Journal file

LAST MONTH: The flag above the Elephant Palace at John Ascuaga's Nugget was lowered in memory of Bertha.

choosing Fort Worth, he said.

Angel's departure will be the end of an era. The Nugget has had an elephant performing in its Celebrity Showroom since 1962, when John Ascuaga purchased Bertha from a circus museum in Wisconsin. Angel came to the Nugget 10 years ago from Busch Gardens in Tampa, Fla.

The Ascuaga family decided it would be too difficult to get another elephant to keep Angel company.

Angel has been doing well since Bertha's death, Ascuaga said. She has been eating and exercising normally. The University of California at Davis has yet to release Bertha's autopsy results or her ashes, he said. The resort hotel is still deciding where to bury Bertha and what kind of a memorial to build for her.

Inside today

Nugget, fans mourn Bertha's death

At age 48: Elephant dies quietly after month of deteriorating health.

By Mike Henderson
RENO GAZETTE-JOURNAL

Bertha the elephant, who gave joy to countless thousands of children and adults, died quietly Wednesday morning in the Elephant Palace at John Ascuaga's Nugget, age 48.

Bertha was nearby.

Angel, Bertha's elephant companion for the past decade, was nearby.

"She actually witnessed Bertha's passing," Stephen Ascuaga said. He said Angel was not eating as well Wednesday as she usually does. Her condition will be monitored and she will be medicated if ap-

"She was such a special animal. There won't be another one. Everybody feels like they had the best dog in the world; I feel like I had the best elephant.

"She'll be a big loss to the community and all the school kids. She was a real favorite."

He said he was aware that Bertha suffered from arthritis, and when she became ill during the past few weeks, the Nugget brought in a veterinarian from Portland and con-

ailments from time to time and had been contacted again in the past few weeks as her health declined.

Stephen Ascuaga, John Ascuaga's son, called Bertha "an elegant lady" and said her health had been deteriorating rapidly since her retirement last month. She was scheduled

PAGE 11A

Opinion: Bertha was part of the community and she will be missed.

Marilyn Newton/Reno Gazette-Journal file

HAPPY DAYS: Bertha shares a moment with one of her trainers, David Loria, in September.

See **BERTHA** on 3A

Bertha

From page 1A

to go to UC-Davis for examination and observation Wednesday but died before she could make the trip, he said.

Her remains will be taken to UC-Davis for limited examination to determine cause of death and for research, he said.

"Bertha had a history of systemic arthritis as is common with Asian elephants and developed problems incident to her age that caused her to deteriorate over the past 72 hours," said Dr. Ren Johnson, a Reno veterinarian.

John Ascuaga said he has no immediate plans to get another elephant; however, the Nugget has been working for six months to acquire the services of a bull elephant to breed with Angel, now 11. A condition of obtaining Angel from Busch Gardens in Tampa was that she would be bred.

John Ascuaga acquired Bertha in 1962 for $8,000 from a circus museum in Wisconsin. He brought her here as a symbol of what was then his Circus Showroom, later renamed the Celebrity Showroom.

There, she was the opening act for or shared billing with such headliners as Red Skelton, Liberace, Jimmy Durante and Tennessee Ernie Ford, all deceased.

"Now another star is gone," John Ascuaga said. "I look back to 1962, and there are not too many entertainers who can say they've performed on the same stage for 37 years."

Bertha was a perennial favorite with schoolchildren, who often took field trips to the Elephant Palace. She and Angel frequently appeared in local parades, and the elephants sometimes would go to visit children at schools. Bertha's last school appearance was in Smith Valley, John Ascuaga said.

The elephant through the years became an icon symbolizing the Nugget. The gift shop Wednesday was stocked with several sizes of plush elephants and an elephant adorns T-shirts for adults and chil-

dren.

In a gift shop window Wednesday, a videocassette called "Tons of Talent — A Day in the Life of Bertha and Angel" was playing continuously.

The video showed Bertha spraying water on people gathered outside the Elephant Palace, the two elephants cavorting in a pool filled with water, Angel following Bertha with her trunk wrapped around Bertha's tail, Bertha with a paintbrush in her trunk painting a picture, and Bertha's trainer putting oversized tap shoes on her feet.

Michonne Ascuaga, 38, who is John Ascuaga's daughter and chief executive officer at the Nugget,

and Stephen Ascuaga, 31, grew up with an elephant in the family.

Michonne Ascuaga recalled childhood Halloweens when she was in costume and put on Bertha's back. She said she was amazed at how well-behaved Bertha was at the Nugget's annual rib cook-off and when surrounded with up to 300 children.

Stephen Ascuaga said Bertha would sometimes seem to get a mischievous glint in her eye.

"She'd kind of lure people up close to her and then she'd spray them with water from her trunk," he said.

He recalled that when he first went to school, one of his classmates reported to his mother: "I've got a friend named Steve Ascuaga, and he's got a pet elephant."

The Nugget for years has had a fan club for the elephants, and members would receive a birthday card each year from the elephants, who ostensibly "signed" the greeting with a footprint.

Michonne Ascuaga said many

birthday greeting recipients are in their 60s.

William Magrath III, now a sophomore at Stanford University in Palo Alto, Calif., recalled that a couple of years ago he was a finalist in the Nugget's college scholarship competition.

"I got this letter from the Nugget, and my parents and I were so excited because we thought we were getting a letter saying I'd won the scholarship.

"It turned out to be a birthday card from Bertha and Angel. I've been getting those forever."

Later, he said he was named the finalist and received a $1,000 Nugget scholarship.

"We used to go out there all the time and watch them playing in the water and in their house," Magrath said.

"I'm sorry she's gone. She was a great elephant."

BERTHA FILE

Name: Bertha, the World's Most Talented Performing Elephant
Age: 48
Place of birth: India
Weight: At one time, more than 5 tons. After dieting, about 4 tons
Weight at birth: About 200 pounds
Cause of death: Undetermined
Life expectancy of an Indian elephant: Up to 50 to 60 years
Diet: Vegetarian, including hay, lettuce, carrots, grain.
First performance at the Nugget: June 28, 1962
Television performances: Ed Sullivan Show, Steve Allen Show, Dinah Shore Show
Talents: Performing "Twinkle, Twinkle Little Star" on an oversized keyboard, dancing to "Baby Elephant Walk," painting while wearing a beret, lifting celebrities, showgirls and others with her trunk
Partial list of celebrities with whom Bertha appeared: Pearl Bailey, Glen Campbell, Diahann Carroll, Carol Channing, Roy Clark, Jimmy Durante, Tennessee Ernie Ford, Crystal Gayle, Andy Griffith, Liberace, Shirley MacLaine, Louise Mandrell, Donald O'Connor, Tony Orlando, Juliet Prowse, Debbie Reynolds, Rowan and Martin, Dinah Shore, Red Skelton, Danny Thomas, Mel Tillis, Ben Vereen, Raquel Welch, Andy Williams.

NUGGET MOURNS: The flag above the Elephant Palace at John Ascuaga's Nugget was lowered in memory of Bertha, who died Wednesday.

Tim Dunn
Reno Gazette-Journal

Happy Birthday From Your Biggest Friends!

Above: As a member of the Bertha fan club you received a birthday greeting from Bertha and Angel.

Events & Gaming

Choose your own adventure with John Ascuaga's Nugget.

Above: Michonne and Stephen Ascuaga pictured with Roger Trounday who was a Nugget gaming executive for 15 years. (2004)

Above: John Ascuaga's "Perfect" slot machines. *Photo by Richard Stokes.*

The year was 1955. Diners in a modest café enjoyed blue-plate specials to the tunes of clinking coins from a handful of slot machines.

Three years later, a casino emerged — one with a few slot machines and an equally small number of table games such as basic blackjack, roulette and craps.

Fast-forward almost five decades to a dramatic contrast, from a casino that got its start with only a limited offering of games to its current presence as one of the region's most diverse recreation destinations. John Ascuaga's Nugget now boasts 47 table games and more than 1,400 slot machines.

The Nugget's expansive casino has a story to tell, with exciting music and laughter serving as the words and glowing neon and flashing

Above: Last Chance Joe awaits a lucky contestant for the silver grab. (1958)

Right: Bart Bosco began working at Dick Graves' Nugget in December of 1955 as a keno writer. Bosco continued to work his way up in the gaming department and after 50 years he still hosts slot tournaments at the Nugget. Next to John, Bart Bosco is one of the Nugget's longest employees. (2000)

lights adding texture to the pictures. Visitors are treated to a choose-your-own-adventure, a pulse-pounding experience that includes slots, video poker, roulette, craps, pai gow poker, bingo, blackjack, keno and more.

The excitement on the casino floor is matched by a line-up of the best promotions offered in the region. John Ascuaga's Nugget has given away millions of dollars in cash, cars, boats — even homes — in promotions that have earned the property a reputation as

Top Right: Last Chance Joe and his burro in a Sparks parade in 1958.

Bottom Right: The winner of a Jeep in the 1959 Nugget Deer Contest.

An avid outdoorsman, John Ascuaga has always enjoyed hunting, fishing and ranching. To celebrate his love of hunting, John came up with the concept of the Hunters' Sweepstakes. The hunter who brought in the largest deer won a brand-new Jeep, the perfect outdoorsman vehicle. Once again John produced a world-class promotion that was unique and innovative.

the party destination. At the Nugget, popular promotions from previous decades often experience a renaissance: Action Ball and Hunt for Cash, for example — both favorites from the '60s — recently named a series of new winners.

Tournaments also are a property highlight: slots, blackjack, poker, bingo — even tourneys exclusively reserved for John's Club members. The Nugget's popular players' club offers card-holders special invitations to events and cash rewards for use in the hotel/casino.

The games are diverse; the opportunities for fun immense; and the surroundings, glowing with electricity. John Ascuaga's Nugget offers a virtual kaleidoscope of recreation set against a backdrop of neon ... a marked contrast from those first few slot machines adorning a humble café.

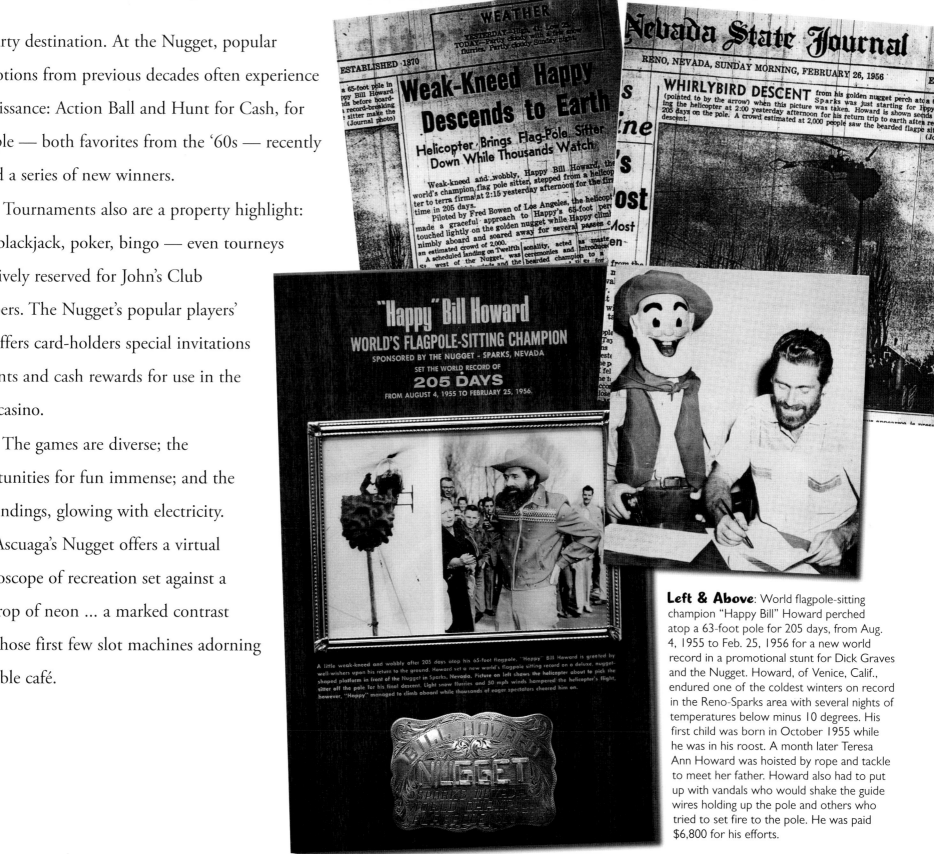

WEATHER
YESTERDAY—High 41, Low 25.
TODAY—Partly cloudy with a few snow flurries. Partly cloudy Sunday night.

ESTABLISHED 1870

Weak-Kneed Happy Descends to Earth
Helicopter Brings Flag-Pole Sitter Down While Thousands Watch

Weak-kneed and wobbly, Happy Bill Howard, the world's champion, flag pole sitter, stepped from a helicopter to terra firma at 2:15 yesterday afternoon for the first time in 205 days.

Piloted by Fred Bowen of Los Angeles, the helicopter made a graceful approach to Happy's 65-foot perch, touched lightly on the golden nugget while Happy climbed nimbly aboard and soared away for several passes over an estimated crowd of 2,000.

A scheduled landing on Twelfth St. west of the Nugget, was ...

Nevada State Journal
RENO, NEVADA, SUNDAY MORNING, FEBRUARY 26, 1956   EST

WHIRLYBIRD DESCENT
from his golden nugget perch at a 65-
(pointed to by the arrow) when this picture was taken. Howard is shown sending the helicopter at 2:00 yesterday afternoon for his return trip to earth after record 205 days on the pole. A crowd estimated at 2,000 people saw the bearded flagpole sitter descent.

"Happy" Bill Howard
WORLD'S FLAGPOLE-SITTING CHAMPION
SPONSORED BY THE NUGGET - SPARKS, NEVADA
SET THE WORLD RECORD OF
205 DAYS
FROM AUGUST 4, 1955 TO FEBRUARY 25, 1956.

A little weak-kneed and wobbly after 205 days atop his 65-foot flagpole, "Happy" Bill Howard is greeted by well-wishers upon his return to the ground. Howard set a new world's flagpole sitting record on a deluxe, nugget-shaped platform in front of the Nugget in Sparks, Nevada. Picture on left shows the helicopter about to pick the sitter off the pole for his final descent. Light snow flurries and 50 mph winds hampered the helicopter's flight, however, "Happy" managed to climb aboard while thousands of eager spectators cheered him on.

BILL HOWARD
NUGGET
SPARKS NEVADA
WORLD CHAMPION

Left & Above: World flagpole-sitting champion "Happy Bill" Howard perched atop a 63-foot pole for 205 days, from Aug. 4, 1955 to Feb. 25, 1956 for a new world record in a promotional stunt for Dick Graves and the Nugget. Howard, of Venice, Calif., endured one of the coldest winters on record in the Reno-Sparks area with several nights of temperatures below minus 10 degrees. His first child was born in October 1955 while he was in his roost. A month later Teresa Ann Howard was hoisted by rope and tackle to meet her father. Howard also had to put up with vandals who would shake the guide wires holding up the pole and others who tried to set fire to the pole. He was paid $6,800 for his efforts.

John Ascuaga was very proud of his Basque heritage. Dick Graves' wife was also very proud of her Basque heritage. To celebrate, they sponsored the Western Basque Festival in 1959. At the time the two-day celebration was the biggest gathering of Basques, their families and friends ever held in the West. Guests of honor included the ambassador of Spain and France, numerous diplomatic, state and city officials including Nevada Governor Grant Sawyer. Five thousand people attended the event and enjoyed Basque food, dancing, a tug-of-war competition between sheepherders and cattlemen and a weight lifting competition.

Dancing sisters. Diana and Delphina Urresti of Boise, Idaho.

Chairman Peter Echeverria and Governor Grant Sawyer greet Ambassador Jose Maria de Areilza of Spain.

Lawrence Welk has been a participant in Nugget Classics for many years. Ah, one, an' a two, an' a par three.

Goldie Hawn was appearing in the Circus Room during the 1968 Classic. She's happy about the winning ticket she just called for a mink coat.

Ready for a test drive are Washoe County Golf Course Pro Pete Marich; Eddie Jones, pro at Hidden Valley Country Club; Pete Carr, Nugget General Manager; and George Bayer, Incline Village Golf Course pro.

Dick Martin laughs in at registration and tries on his Classic Golf hat. Martin and Dan Rowan performed for golfers in the Circus Room.

In 1963, the first Nugget Golf Classic was held. This tournament ran for 14 years and in 1972 was named by Golf Digest magazine as one of the top, best known, amateur fun tournaments in the nation. The star-studded tournament featured celebrities such as Joe DiMaggio, Lawrence Welk, Bob Newhart, Jimmy Durante and George Burns. At one time, the famed tournament had a waiting list of 700.

1966

Charlie Gepford and pro golfer Tony Lima (de were guests at the 1966 Nugget Classic.

That's admiration in f George Burns as ratulates Rolland r his hole-in-one.

1970

John Ascuaga and the golfing padre's close friend Arnold Palmer congratulate the winner.

1972

Lefty Gomez, one of baseball's all-time greats, has been a participant of the Nugget Classic from the beginning years.

at your own level of skill; e bounteous social activities aft. golfing hours; are a fount of new friendships and sometimes business contacts, and — if their popularity is a safe guide — are obviously just one big ball of fun.

Perhaps the best-known of the individual tournaments are the Nugget Classic, in Reno/Sparks, Nev., and the Life Begins at 40 tournament in Harlingen, Tex. The Nugget currently has a waiting list of 700. The Over-40s are always heavily oversubscribed, but fill the field by picking from the hat after regulars have en placed. Tops among the team ament players are in Bern

ne named the Nugget Classic amateur fun tournaments in the 's still a waiting list!

TOURNAMENT HIGHLIGHTS... 1963

The first Nugget Classic Golf Tournament was highlighted with notable personalities. Gathering for the first official photograph were from left, Carl Ravazza (deceased), Lee Francovich, Joe DiMaggio, John Ascuaga, Charles Gepford, and Lefty O'Doul (deceased).

Tournament publicity has always been appealing. Nugget showgirl Stephanie Loren helps publicize the first Nugget Classic.

1973

Pretty Nugget hostess Carla Marquardt holds one of the specially-designed prizes for the closest-to-the-hole awards. This unique device frames the 1972 Thunderbird, hole-in-one prize.

Only a few of the many, many prizes awarded at the Nugget Classic in 1972.

It was instant admiration from the ladies for Peter Marshall. The host of Hollywood Squares charmed everyone, sang, told stories and gave away prizes during one of the luncheons.

Above: Ernie Nevers with John Ascuaga at the 1964 Nugget Classic.

Near Right: Jimmy Durante does some sand-blasting at the Nugget Classic in 1969 as John Ascuaga and Pete Carr watch.

Far Right: "A one and a two ..." Lawrence Welk and John Ascuaga at the 1975 Nugget Golf Classic.

1964
NUGGET
Classic

Left: Joe DiMaggio runs into an elephant hazard at the Nugget Golf Classic.

Near Below: Participants in the Nugget Classic received lavish gifts including shoes, clubs and fur coats.

Far Below: John Ascuaga gets help with his tee shot from former 49ers head coach Dick Nolan at the 1975 Nugget Golf Classic.

Near Right: The John's Club Card featured self-comping for guests.

Far Right: An advertisement for Catch a Y2K Bug (VW) for the new millenium.

For many years, the Nugget celebrated its birth-day on March 17 by giving one lucky customer a huge gift; a brand new three bedroom two car garage home. The wildly successful promotion was a first for the area and once again solidified the Nugget as an innovator in promotions. The Home Sweet Home Sweepstakes attracted thousands of hopeful homeowners from around the country. The last home given away cost $165,000, making it a very generous gift to the winner.

30—Reno Gazette-Journal Wednesday, January 17, 1996

WIN A $163,000 LEWIS HOME FREE

ENTER TODAY AT 8 p.m.

Lewis Homes   COUNTRY RIDGE

Imagine winning a 1,607 sq. ft. home with 3 Bedrooms, 2 Baths, Separate Dining Area, Family Room, Breakfast Nook, Laundry Room, 3-Car Garage.

ENTER FREE
every day at the Home Sweet Home display in the casino.
• Drawing for cash and key held at 8 p.m. daily, Jan. 18 - 16, 1996.
• daily winner receives cash and a certificate key.
• lucky key out of 60 will the door and win the
Win $30,000 cash prizes FREE!

PLUS
EXTRA CHANCES TO WIN!
With an EXTRA DRAWING TICKET with any
• Blackjack
• $25 or more Jackpot
• $10 or more Keno win
• 3 of-a-kind or better in the Poker Room
• Any Bingo game win
FREE!

NTER FREE TODAY!
Days to enter, 60 chances to win! rand Prize Drawing March 17
Complete Sweepstakes rules and details at Home Sweet Home display in the casino.

John Ascuaga's **Nugget**

Leave nothing to chance.

Sparks woman wins $155,000 Reno home

■ **Husband ecstatic:** 'This is a dream come true, unbelievable,' he says.

By Scott Thomsen
GAZETTE-JOURNAL

Jennifer Lee of Sparks had the luck of the Irish with her Wednesday as she won a $155,000 house in west Reno in the Home Sweet Home Sweepstakes at John Ascuaga's Nugget.

"This is a dream come true, unbelievable," her husband Richard Lee said after the couple leapt to the Rose Ballroom stage to collect the prize. "My heart's just boom, boom, boom."

Jennifer Lee qualified for the drawing by winning several slot jackpots greater than $25.

"I play all the time, everyday," she said. She was one of about

38,000 people who entered the contest.

About 800 people in a standing-room-only crowd packed the ball-room Wednesday night for a last chance to become one of the 58 finalists from as far away as Portland, Ore., and Sun City, Ariz. Others watched and listened to the contest on monitors throughout the casino. Finalists had to attend to claim their prizes.

Each finalist won $500 and the chance to draw at least one of 60 numbered house keys from a barrel. Jennifer Lee had won three chances at the prize.

Casino owner John Ascuaga then spun a giant green, white and yellow wheel of fortune that came to rest on Jennifer Lee's lucky number 18.

Their new, 2,000-square-foot house was built by Lewis Homes.

"I went out and looked at this home, it's just beautiful," Ascuaga said. "It might be a condition of the winner that I get one bedroom."

"When do we move in? I don't know," Jennifer Lee said. "Anytime."

David Parker/Gazette-Journal

THE HAPPY COUPLE: Richard and Jennifer Lee of Sparks celebrate with Nugget owner John Ascuaga (center) after winning a $155,000 home Wednesday night at the Sparks casino.

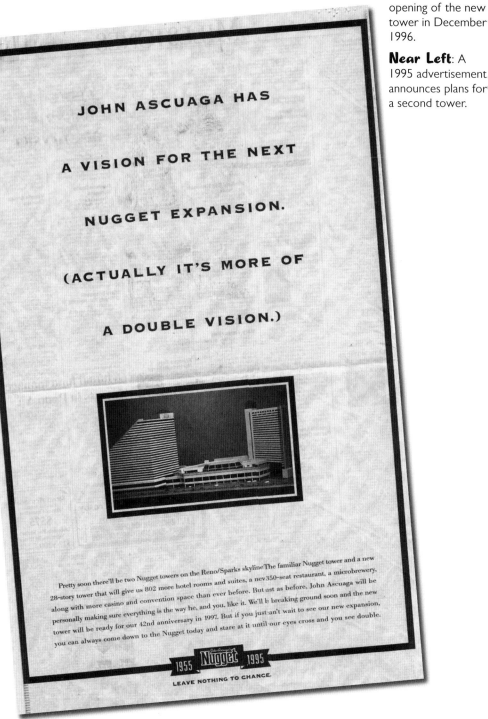

John Ascuaga had a vision. He wanted Sparks to have the biggest and best fireworks show in the Truckee Meadows. He realized this vision in 2000, when John Ascuaga's Nugget, the City of Sparks and many other Sparks businesses came together to put on Star Spangled Sparks on Victorian Square. The event has grown each year, attracting 40,000 locals and tourists to the 2004 spectacular.

Above: An advertisement for Star Spangled Sparks fireworks show in 2000.

In 2000, the Reno-Sparks-Tahoe region offered a plethora of world-class golf courses, but hadn't firmly established itself as a premier golf destination. John Ascuaga's Nugget saw this as an opportunity, and took the lead for the region in establishing the John Ascuaga's Nugget Amateur Challenge. Marketed nationally, this 54-hole handicap event introduced new tourists to the area. At the fifth annual event in 2004, nearly 400 participants came from 39 states and two foreign countries.

Left: John Miceli of Sparks spins the paycheck wheel in June 1984. The Nugget's innovative paycheck promotion gave locals who cashed their paycheck the chance to win cash, drinks and free meals in the restaurants.
Photo by Lance Iversen

Top: Frank Adams was the $60,000 winner of the 1989 Nugget Classic Slot Tournament. Roger Trounday (left) and John L. Ascuaga (right) present the check.

John Ascuaga has always rolled up his sleeves and appeared in his own television commercials. Never afraid to poke fun at himself, the Nugget's commercials have consistently been known for their humor.

Above: A billboard in 1998 on Interstate 80 in Sparks is one of many advertisements using John Ascuaga's face. The billboards made Ascuaga more recognizable to customers in and out of Reno and showed his sense of humor.
Photo by Tim Dunn

Pedometer: John Ascuaga's never-stand still business approach was parodied in his famous pedometer commercial. The 60 second spot began with John placing a pedometer next to his belt buckle at the beginning of his day. Walking around the vast casino in his trademark cowboy boots, John checked all the restaurants, several rooms and chatted with a group of guests in the hotel lobby. At the end of his day when he removed the pedometer it showed that John had walked 7.02 miles. A typical day for John.

Window and Perfect Series: John's hands-on approach to business has been his trademark since opening in 1955. Two memorable commercials that celebrated this approach depicted John as a helpful window washer cleaning the windows of his own hotel. The 'Perfect' commercial, as it has become known, features John tasting the soup in Restaurante Orozko and exclaiming that it's perfect. Then John is featured in the arcade racing a motorcycle and again saying that the game is perfect. Then finally John is seen testing the water in one of the Jacuzzi's at the indoor/outdoor atrium pool while dressed in his suit submerged in the water past his waist. Two guests clad in swimsuits look on with shock and amazement. Again, John proclaims that the temperature of the water is "perfect."

Best in the West Nugget Rib Cook-Off

Above: During the Best in the West Nugget Rib Cook-Off the main stage has nightly free entertainment. (2004)

Above: Tommy Houston from Checkered Pig Barbecue, Martinsville, Virginia, takes top prize in the 2004 Best in the West Nugget Rib Cook-Off and enthusiastically hugs Stephen Ascuaga as the Food Network films his victory.

The Best in the West Nugget Rib Cook-Off was invented to help off-set a typically slow three day weekend in the casino business, Labor Day. Traditionally families camp or barbecue at home on Labor Day, however John and the events staff at the Nugget decided that if you invited the best rib cookers in the country to a rib cook-off with cash prizes people would forego their backyard barbecues and come to the Nugget. The concept took off and now 16 years later the Best in the West Nugget Rib Cook-Off features 24 of the best rib cookers and over 300,000 rib enthusiasts descend on Victorian Square to feast for five days. In 2004, 154,000 pounds of pork ribs were consumed, making the Best in the West Nugget Rib Cook-Off the largest barbecue in the world.

David B. Parker/Reno Gazette-Journal

WINNER: Jim Clayton of the Texas Outlaw Barb-B-Que Team of Elizabethtown, Ky., carries a trophy and a pig-shaped check worth $7,500, back to his stand Monday after winning the Best in the West Nugget Rib Cook-off in Sparks.

Cook-off a rib-tickling success

Winner claims top prize, trophy for the third time

By Lenita Powers
RENO GAZETTE-JOURNAL

Texas Outlaw Barb-B-Que won first place Monday at the 15th annual Best in the West Nugget Rib Cook-off in Sparks, making it the boss hog of barbecue at the cook-off for three out of the last four years.

"This has to be — next to the day my daughter was born — the best day of my life," Jim Clayton, owner of the Texas Outlaw restaurant in Elizabethtown, Ky., said as he claimed his trophy and $7,500 prize.

Although "totally euphoric" over his third first-place win in the cook-off, Clayton said there are no losers because the competitors who come to Sparks by invitation only are the best in the world.

"I've won just about every major competition in North America, and this is the hardest of them all," he said. "Of the 20 or so competitions I go to every year, I would take one win here over 10 at the other cook-offs."

Frankie Vigil, publicist for John Ascuaga's Nugget,

said the five-day event drew an estimated 300,000 people who devoured more than 130,000 pounds of ribs.

Sparks resident Brian Janes and his family were

among them.

Janes said he and his wife, Brady, went to the cook-off with their two sons, Jake, 5, and Neil, 3, almost every day.

"It's very family-oriented," said Brady Janes, 30. "They have stuff for the kids to do and there's the (Sparks theater) fountain and all the food. They've done a great job keeping things clean, too."

See **RIBS** on **4C**

RESULTS

Rib cook-off winners:
1st: Texas Outlaw Barb-B-Que, Elizabethtown, Ky.
2nd: Kinder's Custom Meats, Concord, Calif.
3rd: Bone Daddy's, Midland, Mich.
4th: Arizona Barbecue, Phoenix
5th: Sweet Meat Cooking Team, Euless, Texas
People's Choice Award: Carson City BBQ
Best Sauce: Kinder's Custom Meats

BEST in THE WEST NUGGET RIB COOK-OFF 2003

Ribs/Sparks Labor Day event wraps up

From **1C**

The Janes family had been rooting for their favorite rib cooker, B.J.'s Barbecue in Sparks, but their hometown favorite didn't place this year.

But the People's Choice Award did go to a Nevada company: Carson City BBQ, owned by Duane Felker and Phil Hyatt.

"We know the people like our ribs, so we'll keep trying," Felker said of continuing the quest for the top prize.

Felker said Carson City BBQ won both the Best Sauce and the

People's Choice awards in 2001.

Although the business only does catering, Felker said its barbecue sauce is available in some stores, including Raley's supermarkets in Reno, Carson City and Gardnerville.

Dan Kinder, owner of Kinder's Custom Meats in Concord, Calif., won $3,000 and second place this year as well as $500 for the Best Sauce Award.

"Right after the announcement, we sold out of sauce," Kinder said. "We got slammed. In about 40 minutes,

we sold 150 bottles."

Kinder said he felt good about taking second place in the overall competition against some of the country's top rib cookers.

"I'm totally tickled because I'm competing against professional people. I'm a butcher by trade. I have a deli and a butcher shop, but I don't consider myself a professional," he said.

"I just love to cook, and this is something I wanted to master so I could try and compete with the big boys, even though I don't consider myself one of the big boys."

Best Bets

Get sauced

Best in the West Nugget Rib Cook-Off attracts top competitors

Pages 27-30

Above: Anna Miller, who was age 1 1/2 when her picture was taken at the 1998 Rib Cook-Off, graces the cover of the Reno Gazette-Journal's entertainment news magazine, which previewed the 1999 competition. *Photo by Marilyn Newton*

Marilyn Newton/Gazette-Journal

TOPS: Hubert Green, left, and the winning crew from Sweet Meat.

Nugget tickled by rib cook-off success

By Jill Jorden/Gazette-Journal

After four days of meat-munching and sauce-slurping, organizers of the Best of the West Nugget Rib Cook-off dished out $11,000 in prize money Monday as the event drew to a close.

All told, the cook-off, sponsored by John Ascuaga's Nugget, attracted 16 competitors and more than 50,000 hungry Labor Day celebrants. Organizers said it was so successful they plan to make it an annual event.

"It was awesome," said Ben Plaza, Nugget special events director. "It far exceeded our expectations."

The cook-off began Friday afternoon and ran daily through Monday afternoon on Sparks' Victorian Square. Competitors came from restaurants in Nevada, California, Texas, Oregon, Washington, Arkansas and Illinois.

The following prizes were awarded Monday afternoon:

☐ The $5,000 first-place award went to Sweet Meat of Euless, Texas.

☐ Second prize, $2,500, went to Sutphens Ribs of Amarillo, Texas.

☐ Third prize, $1,000, was awarded to Down Home Ribs of Antioch, Calif.

☐ The $2,500 award for best sauce

See RIB, page 2C

Rib cook-off

From page 1C
was given to Armadillo Willy's, a Los Altos, Calif., restaurant that bills itself "The Best Little Ribhouse *not* in Texas."

Hubert Green, co-owner of Sweet Meat, said the secret to his success is a special combination of spices — he won't say which — and a lot of patience.

"We cook 'em slow, for five hours," Green said. "They're hickory smoked — no heat under the meat, ever.

"That way, they come off good and tender."

So good and tender, he said, that customers willingly plan their culinary schedules around Sweet Meat's limited hours. The restaurant is open for Friday lunch and Saturday dinner. Period.

And that's just the way Green and his partners want it. They spend the rest of their time catering and occasionally packing their 5-foot metal armadillo for a rib cook-off.

Green said he'll use the prize money to promote his business, but not to expand it.

"We're happy the way we are," he said. "We've just got a good product that people like."

Top: Kyle Webster, 8 in 2001, shows off his chops after finishing his meal at the Best in the West Nugget Rib Cook-Off. *Photo by Andy Barron*

Top Right: Rib and sauce cook Phil Hyatt stands in front of his booth at the 2001 Rib Cook-off, offering Carson City BBQ Co. Stickers to rib fans at the festival. *Photo by Andy Barron*

Bottom Left: An overview of Victorian Square in 1997, with bandstand, tents and the crowd in front of the Nugget at the Best in the West Nugget Rib Cook-Off.

Bottom Right: Paul Mackay gets some help from his wife, Karen, in carrying the winning trophy for the 2001 Rib Cook-Off back to the Aussom Aussie booth. *Photo by David B. Parker*

Top Left: Jim Clayton of Texas Outlaws Barbecue Team out of Elizabethtown, Ky., proudly lifts his 2002 first-place Rib Cook-Off trophy just given to him by Stephen Ascuaga, right, on stage at Victorian Square. Clayton also won top honors at th 2003 Cook-Off, making him the only back-to-back winner of the prestigious event. *Photo by Candice Towell.*

Middle Left: This armadillo rib cooker caught the attention of visitors to the 1997 Best in the West Nugget Rib Cook-Off. *Reno Gazette-Journal library.*

Above: Ivery Grays of Los Banos, Calif., cooks ribs at the 1997 Best in the West Nugget Rib Cook-Off. *Photo by Mark Studyvin.*

Left: Leah Ciogani, right, fights off the tears while co-worker Kandy Miller works on giant onions for Gary's World Famous Foods of Cleveland at the 1997 Rib Cook-Off. *Photo by Tim Dunn.*

Bull Sale

A ton of talent on stage has been a mooving tradition at the Nugget.

Above: A young admirer with a prize bull up for auction at the 1980 bull sale. *Reno Gazette-Journal library*

When the curtain rises in the Nugget's Celebrity Showroom, guests prepare for the very best in entertainment. They prepare for an unforgettable evening highlighted by big names, immense talent and larger-than-life performances.

And the show promises never to disappoint — especially when the talent literally weighs a ton and boasts a name like Bessie.

Stars of the bovine variety grace center stage every year at John Ascuaga's Nugget for the Western Nugget National Hereford Show and Sale, a gathering of the finest pedigreed Herefords and their owners. Nugget owner John Ascuaga has demonstrated his love for ranching — he raises Herefords at his Jack's Valley Ranch near Carson City — providing a venue for the event since 1969. During the show and sale, bulls and heifers replace traditional

This Photo: A prize bull parade crosses B Street in 1974. Reno Gazette-Journal library

headliner entertainment in the Celebrity Showroom for the only bull sale in the world to be held in a casino.

Herefords are known as the finest cows on the range, producing more calves per cow than most other breeds and also boasting a high "conversion factor" — the number of pounds of feed it takes to produce a pound of protein on the animal. The prestige of their breeding in turn earns them a prestigious price tag; many go for tens of thousands of dollars.

The annual event is reminiscent of teen talent shows and beauty pageants — only with a decidedly auction-oriented twist. Hereford owners spend hours with vacuums, blow dryers, glitter and combs, primping and preening in the tradition of proud pageant parents.

And the results are phenomenal, with breeders often from thousands of miles away sometimes shelling out thousands of dollars for the blue-blooded bulls and heifers.

Big names? Definitely. Big talent? The breeders would certainly say so. Just plain big? Absolutely. Audiences at the Nugget's annual Hereford cattle show and sale would agree that these big bovines are the ultimate show-stoppers.

Top: A packed house watches at the 1977 Hereford Herd Bull sale. *Photo by Harry Upson*

Bottom: Bidding during the 1972 Hereford Herd Bull Sale is rapid as the prize-winning animals are paraded before prospective customers on the Celebrity Showroom stage.

Above: Bulls and their handlers are lined up on the Celebrity Showroom stage in 1979.

Community

While most casinos boast of big winners at blackjack tables and slot machines, John Ascuaga's Nugget has a slightly different approach: Its winners not only are found on the casino floor, but also in local high schools or representing arts organizations, softball teams and Girl Scout Troops. Reflecting its owner's personal commitment to giving to the community that has embraced the business for years, the Nugget routinely donates manpower, money and resources to charitable causes.

Perhaps its most well-known contribution goes annually to local high school students. Since 1956, the Nugget has contributed nearly a half-million dollars to almost 500 high school and community college students. The $1,000 scholarships were first awarded to four students — two from Reno and two from Carson City. Now, 50 years later, 24 students from high schools throughout northern Nevada and

Above: Michonne Ascuaga and her brother, Stephen, stand with "The Spirit of Sparks," a bighorn sheep that was one of 25 different painted sheep displayed throughout Reno-Sparks as part of the 2002 Artown festivities — a celebration of the arts in Reno-Sparks. *Photo by Marilyn Newton.*

Right: President Reagan with John L., Michonne and John Ascuaga.

two minority students receive Nugget scholarships.

A pictorial retrospective graces a wall outside the Nugget's Rotisserie restaurant, reflections of the hundreds of young lives personally touched by generous scholarships over the years.

But Nugget donations often are about more than money; time and personal assistance sometimes send even stronger messages, which is why the Nugget encourages employees to donate their time each Thanksgiving and Christmas. Annually since 1955, the Nugget has provided and served holiday meals at St. Vincent's Dining Room, a local mission.

And personal missions also have inspired donations, like that of Michonne Ascuaga, John's daughter and the Nugget's chief executive officer. She has translated her passion for the arts into numerous contributions in support of the Sierra Arts Foundation, Nevada Museum of Art, Youth Art Works and the City of Reno-sponsored Artown Celebration.

Some casinos measure success in terms of wins and losses, but John Ascuaga's Nugget focuses on its winners: half a century worth of lives and causes it has assisted through contributions to the community.

Right: Autographed poster to John Ascuaga from Nobel laureate Bishop Desmond Tutu, who appeared at John Ascuaga's Nugget.

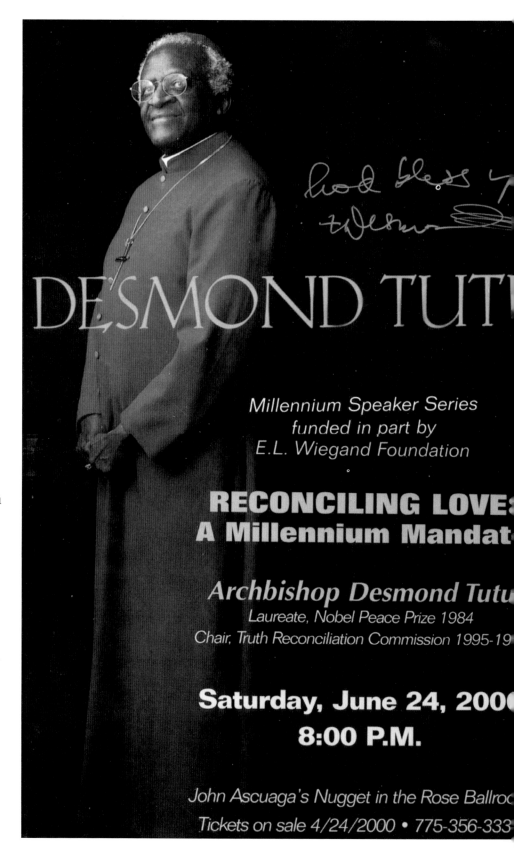

DESMOND TUTU

Millennium Speaker Series
funded in part by
E.L. Wiegand Foundation

**RECONCILING LOVE:
A Millennium Mandate**

Archbishop Desmond Tutu
Laureate, Nobel Peace Prize 1984
Chair, Truth Reconciliation Commission 1995-19

**Saturday, June 24, 2000
8:00 P.M.**

John Ascuaga's Nugget in the Rose Ballroom
Tickets on sale 4/24/2000 • 775-356-333

Left: John Ascuaga chats with recipients of his scholarship at the annual Nugget Scholarship Luncheon in 1999. On his right is Dana Fenili of Smith Valley High School. The Nugget has been distributing scholarships to college-bound high school seniors since 1956. More than 500 northern Nevada students have received scholarships. *Photo by Marilyn Newton*

Near Left: Elizabeth Lightfoot, left, of Sparks High School, is joined by Joseph Mahsman of Spanish Springs High and Karen Kaufmann of Reed High as three of John Ascuaga's 2004 Scholarship winners. *Photo by Bel Willem*

Below: John Ascuaga with 2004 Scholarship recipients.

Above: John Ascuaga is a firm believer in education, and has contributed over $500,000 to college-bound northern Nevada high school graduates over the years. *Photo by Richard Stokes*

Celebrities

Over the years the Nugget has had the opportunity to host and entertain some of the biggest names in entertainment, sports and politics, including United States Presidents and Nevada Governors. Often times John Ascuaga was on hand to welcome his famous guests and was always available for a quick photo. Known for his sense of humor, John often was photographed with celebrities in tongue and cheek poses. These priceless photos chronicle not only the Nugget's history, but also that of music, television, sports and politics.

Above: John Ascuaga gives Mitch Miller a spin about town in 1965.

Left: Portrait photo of Red Skelton. Red performed at the Nugget hundreds of times and was a close personal friend of John Ascuaga. Several of Red's clown paintings still hang in John's office.

This Photo: Red Skelton gets a big kick out of John Ascuaga dancing with the president of the Snaffle Bit Futurity.

Right: Then-Texas Governor George W. Bush with John Ascuaga (2000).

Left: Notre Dame football Coach Lou Holtz chats with John Ascuaga at a University of Nevada, Reno fundraiser.

Below: Evangelist Billy Graham and John Ascuaga.

Above: Then-Vice President George H.W. Bush with John Ascuaga in 1982.

Right: Wilt Chamberlain gives John Ascuaga a boost in 1962.

Left: Is it pachyderm pugilism with John Ascuaga squaring off with boxing champion Gene Fullmer in 1963?

Far Above: Roy Clark unwraps a gift from John Ascuaga in 1970.

Near Above: Comedian Bob Newhart, left, Bertha, and trumpet player Al Hirt were on hand for the Nugget Golf Classic in 1969.

Left & Above: Lorne Greene from the hit television show Bonanza poses for publicity shots with John Ascuaga. The Nugget hosted the cast of Bonanza many times. (1966)

Above: Is he dreaming? John Ascuaga with baseball Hall of Famers Joe DiMaggio, right, and Mickey Mantle, left.

Right: Nevada Gov. Mike O'Callaghan and John Ascuaga in 1977.

Left: John Ascuaga and President Gerald Ford in 1974.

Far Above: John Ascuaga and Vice President Walter Mondale in 1975.

Near Above: Tennessee Ernie Ford and John Ascuaga swap some bull in 1978.

Family

Above: John Ascuaga proudly holds his diploma from the University of Idaho. He graduated in three years with a Bachelor of Science degree in Accounting. A member of Phi Delta Theta, he and his college roommate, Dwight Morrison, are pictured in front of their fraternity house.

Right: The Nugget and John Ascuaga have always been known for giving back to the community. Here John himself gives blood during a blood shortage in 1983.

Opposite: John Ascuaga is seated next to his wife, Rose, and their youngest daughter, Michonne. On the left is Rose's mother, Marie Louise Ardans who is flanked by Camille and John L., John and Rose's oldest daughter and oldest son. The family is celebrating the Nugget's 11th birthday on March 17, 1966.

Integrity ... Dedication ... Family. For John Ascuaga, these three watchwords — and, in particular, family — have come to represent his career and his very essence.

John Ascuaga's father came to America in 1914 from Orozko, Spain, in the Pyrenees Mountains. Jose was a sheepherder who traveled to America with his brother, Pablo. He eventually settled in the tiny Idaho town of Notus. John's mother, Marina, traveled from Spain to join Jose on the family farm, originally 90 acres of brush land.

The couple had four children: Carmen, Frank and, in 1925, John and his twin sister, Rose, were born.

Jose, who like so many Basques was a hard-working and industrious man, stressed the value of education to his four children. John took these early lessons

to heart, and earned his bachelor's degree in accounting after only three-and-a-half years of study at the University of Idaho in Moscow.

Following graduation from Idaho in 1951, John earned his bachelor of arts degree in hotel and restaurant management from nearby Washington State University in Pullman in 1952.

In 1958, John married Rose Ardans. Rose, then a surgical nurse at Saint Mary's Hospital in Reno, is of French Basque heritage. John and Rose have four children, Camille (1959), John (1960), Michonne (1961) and Stephen (1968).

Two of the couple's children are currently involved in the operation of John Ascuaga's Nugget. Daughter Michonne Ascuaga, a 1983 graduate of Santa Clara University and holder of an MBA from

Right: John Ascuaga and Rose Ardans were married at St. Thomas Aquinas Cathedral and followed with an elaborate reception at the Nugget. John and Rose Ascuaga's wedding was attended by 500 guests. (June 15, 1958)

BRIDE

Wedding of Popular Couple Is Followed by Elaborate Reception for Guests

In a setting of white gladioli, blue delphinium and soft candlelight, the marriage of Miss Rose L. Ardans and John J. Ascuaga was solemnized June 15 at 4 p.m. in St. Thomas Aquinas Cathedral.

Msgr. Robert Anderson officiated at the nuptial mass, witnessed by family members and close friends of the couple.

Mrs. Emil Tolotti presided at the organ, providing appropriate nuptial music which included "The Lord's Prayer" and "Ave Maria."

Given in marriage by her brother, Rene Ardans, the bride was regal in her wedding gown of delustered satin featuring a high scoop neckline and short sleeves. The hand-tucked satin of the bodice displayed the empire line and the sheath front of the gown flowed gracefully into the satin cathedral length train. The pointed band headpiece of matching delustered satin was adorned with a trim of pearl loops and held the double veil of imported illusion. She wore a pearl necklace, gift of her bridegroom and carried a white prayer book topped with Phalaenopsis orchids and lily-of-the-valley tied with satin streamers. Completing her ensemble were long, white kid gloves, the traditional blue garter and a sixpence tucked in her white satin French heeled pumps.

Attendants

Miss Elizabeth O'Driscoll of Reno was maid of honor and bridesmaids were the Misses Margot DeBour and Veronica Sallaberry, both of Reno.

Standing with the bridegroom was Frank Ascagua of Caldwell, Ida., and doing usher duty were Paul Araguistain of Cleveland, Ohio, and Fred Reich of San Francisco, Calif.

The maid of honor and bridesmaids wore sheath gowns of silk organza over taffeta in an exquisite shade of Romance blue. The sleeveless bodices were designed with scoop neckline; inset bands displayed the empire line with draped panel adding back interest to the skirts. Matching headbands, shoes and short white kid gloves completed the outfits. Each wore a strand of pearls, gifts of the bride and they carried cascade bouquets of delphinium blue glamellias.

Mrs. Ardans attended her daughter's wedding in rose lace dress, rose accessories and corsage of white Phalaenopsis orchids. Mrs. Ascagua, mother

of the bridegroom, was in blue lace with blue accessories and corsage of Phalaenopsis orchids.

Reception

Following the ceremony a large reception was held in the Virginian Room of the Sparks Nugget. A profusion of flowers adorned the walls and a latticework arch provided the background for the bride's table, centered with a seven-tiered wedding cake. The base of the cake was wreathed with white gardenias and fern. Several huge punch bowls were carved of ice in which were embedded a colorful array of live carnations while pin wheels of colored light emanated from the base of each bowl.

There was a champagne fountain which cascaded gently over tiers of ice to the base which was wreathed with white gardenias and fern.

Refreshments included a buffet table of hot dishes and long tables of artfully decorated hors d' oeuvres. More than 500 guests attended the reception.

There was a large cake for the bride and bridegroom decorated in a pastoral theme with "congratulations to the Wedding Couple" in Basque, their native tongue.

Mrs. Albert Roth, twin sister of Mr. Ascagua presided at the organ during the reception and Mrs. Richard D. Sheretz was in charge of the guest book.

Mrs. Ascagua is the daughter of Mrs. Leon Ardans and the late Mr. Ardans, formerly of Eureka, Nev. She has been employed at St. Mary's Hospital for the past four years, receiving her training at Holy Cross School of Nursing, Holy Cross Hospital, Salt Lake City.

Mr. Ascagua is the son of Mr. and Mrs. Ascagua of Caldwell, Ida. He attended the University of Idaho and Washington State College before coming to Sparks where he is manager of the Nugget.

When Mr. and Mrs. Ascagua left for the Pacific Northwest on a honeymoon the bride was wearing a beige silk linen suit, beige linen accessories and white orchid corsage.

Out-of-town guests at the wedding and reception included Mr. and Mrs. Jose Ascagua and Mr. and Mrs. Frank Ascagua of Caldwell, Ida.; Mr. and Mrs. Albert Roth of Wapato, Wash.; Mr. and Mrs. James Blackwell of Boise, Ida., and John Harriet of Corning, Calif.

Mr. and Mrs. Ascagua are making their home in Sparks.

Bride of John Ascagua is the former Miss Rose L. Ardans and she is pictured in wedding gown of delustered satin, fashioned on classic lines.

(Ernie M

Stanford University, is chief executive officer. Son Stephen Ascuaga holds a degree in marketing from the University of San Diego. He is the senior executive vice president and oversees the marketing and gaming areas.

Given his family history, it is not surprising that John Ascuaga continues to prefer to live close to the land: he resides on the family's 1,250-acre Jack's Valley Ranch in northern Douglas County.

Right: Formal portrait, 1960.

To the Ascuaga youngsters
Gloria fo Jimmy Durante

Comstock's
THE BUSINESS OF NEVADA

ALL IN THE FAMILY
Successful successions in family business

Competition on Hold
When will phone deregulation lead to lower rates?

Origins of Incline
What makes Incline Village such a prestigious zip code?

John and Michonne Ascuaga

Comstock's Magazine
1300 Terminal Way #202
Reno, NV 89502
Change Service Requested

Left: John, Camille, Michonne and John L. with singing legend and regular performer in the then Circus Room, Jimmy Durante in 1969.

Above: As one of the industry's last family-owned and operated casino/resorts, John and Michonne Ascuaga were featured on the cover of Comstock's Northern Nevada Business Magazine in 1988.

The cake in the right photo reads:

11

1966
WHAT'S NEXT?

1965
CONVENTION CENTER

1963
ROOMETTES

1959
MOTOR LODGE

Hut · Coral · 1958 7th · Pacific · Liquor Store · John Asc

TRADER DICKS

Pancake · Pari · Rooster Room · 1955 · Roundhouse · Red Bar

JOHN ASCUAGA'S NUGGET

THE NUGGET'S 11TH BIRT
AND
ST. PATRICKS DAY CELE

Daily · GUEST
APPEARANCES BY B

WED. THURS
Free
CAKE & CO

5:00 to
Beer
10¢

Wednesda
FIVE "Mon

BIRTH
worth $10

BE
AWAY

8:00

Above: John Ascuaga and his family live on his ranch in Jack's Valley. He scratches his dog, Opie, while astride his horse, Nugget. *Photo by Joe Gosen*

Right: St. Patrick's Day celebration and the Nugget's 11th birthday, 1966.

This Photo: John Ascuaga in his office at the time of the Nugget's 45th anniversary in 2000. *Photo by Andy Barron*

Below: A rancher at heart, John Ascuaga can often be seen wearing a cowboy hat and boots.

Right: John and Rose Ascuaga, July 5, 2003. John and Rose were married on June 15, 1958, after a three-month courtship. John is Spanish Basque, while his bride is French Basque.

Top: John Ascuaga, Stephen Ascuaga and Rick Davenport (center) dine in The Loft, The Nugget's employee restaurant. John can be seen eating with his employees almost daily (2004).

Bottom: CEO Michonne Ascuaga with her father, John, in his office in 2002.

Photo by Marilyn Newton

Right: Nugget CEO Michonne Ascuaga in her office (2004).
Photo by Richard Stokes

Near Below: Stephen and John Ascuaga

Far Below: Nugget CEO Michonne Ascuaga chairs a meeting. At her left are her father, John Ascuaga, and her brother, Stephen Ascuaga (2004). *Photo by Richard Stokes*

.scuaga picks daughter for CEO

FRI OCT 10 1997

Stearns

ETTE-JOURNAL

Ascuaga's Nugget on elevated a family member cutive officer to replace ubbers, ed last 5 years s hotel-

Ascuaga

As-oves to senior vice he be-econd run a casino in northern other is Tracy Mimno-was promoted to gen-of the Peppermill n June.

"She's earned the respect of everyone among our 2,800 employees, so that's something to be proud of," said Michonne's father, John Ascuaga, the Nugget's owner and operator. "I just love her ability—how she relates to everyone, whether it's a maid or one of the vice presidents."

Because Michonne Ascuaga worked closely with Lubbers, she expects a smooth transition. "We have that kind of a team — we're always doing things corroboratively," she said.

Is there added pressure that goes with being an Ascuaga and CEO?

Aside from worrying more and feeling the job is more than a job, "I would have said I had more pressure in the beginning, when I got my first promotion," Michonne Ascuaga said. "I'm not really in the stage where I'm proving myself."

Asked if he had considered anyone else for CEO, John cited her background and answered, "I don't know why."

Michonne Ascuaga brings to the post 14 years of full-time experience at the Nugget, a master's degree in business administration from Stanford University and a bachelor's degree in math and computer science from Santa Clara University. She also studied at the London School of Economics, where she emphasized American, European and international economics.

"Educationally, her foundation can't be surpassed, I don't think," plus she brings common sense and experience, John Ascuaga said.

Peppermill's Mimno-Nichols called Michonne Ascuaga an integral part of the Nugget's success and expects she will "continue to demon-

strate outstanding leadership."

"She has an excellent reputation in the gaming community," Mimno-Nichols said. "We're delighted for her."

Michonne Ascuaga started at the Nugget in 1983, when work began on the east hotel tower. She helped to develop the new west tower that opened in December 1996, bringing the Nugget's room count to 1,661. She also was the Nugget's executive vice president of sales and marketing, and worked in its credit, accounting, marketing and convention sales departments.

She worked summer vacations opening mail at the Nugget's Roof Garden motel starting when she was 13, "when she was so small that she could hardly look over the counter (and) she isn't much bigger now," John Ascuaga joked.

Michonne Ascuaga said the Nugget will be reorganizing different positions during the transition, but the property will stay its course.

"We still have a lot of things we want to do," she said, soonest of which includes completing the Nugget's largest restaurant, Orozko, by spring.

Outside the Nugget, Michonne Ascuaga sits on several boards, including the Reno Air Race Association, Sierra Arts Foundation and Santa Clara University board of regents, and is a former board member of U.S. Bank of Nevada.

She is married to Dr. Kevin Linkus.

Two of three other Ascuaga children also work at the Nugget: Stephen, executive vice president of marketing, and John L., executive vice president of casino operations

Above: The Ascuaga family on August 27, 2004. Back Row: Priscilla Ascuaga holding two-day old Marisol Ascuaga, Rose Ascuaga, John J. Ascuaga, John L. Ascuaga, Michonne Ascuaga, Gabriel Bressler, Camille (Ascuaga) Bressler and Mark Bressler. Front Row: Stephen Ascuaga, Malia Ascuaga, Sean Ascuaga (John L. Ascuaga's son), Rosie Linkus (Michonne's daughter), Dr. Kevin Linkus (Michonne's husband), Miriam Bressler and Noah Bressler.

The Future

John Ascuaga has spent fifty years investing and reinvesting in the Nugget, the city and the region. He has instilled his personal and business principles in his children, Michonne and Stephen. Together with their team at the Nugget, they are committed to the long-term success of the organization and the community.

Chief Executive Officer Michonne Ascuaga has spent countless months working with city government to redevelop and create a more vibrant Downtown Sparks. She has a vision for the future that includes a major entertainment and shopping complex--a development that would help not only the city economy, but become a major tourist destination.

Senior Executive Vice President Stephen Ascuaga has focused much of his attention on helping Northern Nevada develop stronger tourism programs. Through his work with such groups as the Regional Marketing Committee, Reno-Sparks Convention and Visitors Authority and many others, Stephen has helped create and implement marketing programs that attract new visitors to the region.

Both Michonne and Stephen have a strong commitment to John Ascuaga's Nugget. It's hard to say what the Nugget will look like in another 50 years, but you can bet that Michonne and Stephen will be there to make sure it continues to be a first-class organization and destination that cares about its employees, its guests and its community.

Above: John Ascuaga's Nugget Senior Management Team on October 12, 2004. Back Row: Tom Flaherty, Vern Sohrt, Rick Davenport, Steve Gearty and Tom Newell. Front Row: Beth Cooney, Jimmy Chan, Stephen Ascuaga; John Ascuaga, Michonne Ascuaga, Helen O'Brien, Brenda McCarty Lee and Larry Harvey.